DISCOVER THE
HIDDEN YOU

Destiny Image Books by Dr. Myles Munroe

Maximizing Your Potential

In Pursuit of Purpose

Releasing Your Potential

Overcoming Crisis

40 Days to Discovering God's Big Idea

Rediscovering Faith

Rediscovering the Kingdom

Rediscovering Kingdom Worship

Kingdom Principles

Applying the Kingdom

Potential for Every Day

Glory of Living

Purpose and Power of Love and Marriage

Purpose and Power of Praise and Worship

Understanding Your Potential

Myles Munroe 365-Day Devotional & Journal

Single, Married, Separated, and Life After Divorce

Kingdom Parenting

Waiting and Dating

DISCOVER THE
HIDDEN YOU

The Secret to Living the Good Life

DR. MYLES MUNROE

DESTINY IMAGE® PUBLISHERS, INC.
P.O. Box 310, Shippensburg, PA 17257-0310
"Promoting Inspired Lives."

This book and all other Destiny Image and Destiny Image Fiction books are available at Christian bookstores and distributors worldwide.

Cover design by Eileen Rockwell

For more information on foreign distributors, call 717-532-3040.

Reach us on the Internet: www.destinyimage.com.

ISBN 13 TP: 978-0-7684-5796-4

ISBN 13 eBook: 978-0-7684-5794-0

ISBN 13 HC: 978-0-7684-5793-3

ISBN 13 LP: 978-0-7684-5795-7

For Worldwide Distribution, Printed in the U.S.A.

1 2 3 4 5 6 7 8 / 25 24 23 22 21

CONTENTS

1 God, the Source of All 11

2 Omnipotent God 14

3 From Nothingness to Everything 16

4 Then God Said 19

5 A Work in Progress 21

6 Many Look, Few See 24

7 God Sees the Authentic You 27

8 A Worthwhile Somebody 30

9 God Sees All 32

10	A Great Tragedy	35
11	What God Sees in You	38
12	Christ in You	41
13	The Adversary	43
14	The Liar	46
15	Abundant Life	49
16	Strongholds	52
17	Wisdom and You	54
18	Perversions	56
19	God's Secret Wisdom	59
20	But...	61
21	Born of the Spirit	64
22	Holy Spirit Deep Dive	67
23	There Is More	70
24	God's Bucket of Hope	72
25	Feelin' Good	75
26	No Mistakes	78
27	Your Book's Sequel	80
28	To Him Be Glory	82

29	Just Believe, Dummy!	84
30	First a Thought	86
31	Plans and Goals	89
32	Destined by God	92
33	Nothing Named "Can't"	95
34	Determined by Demands	97
35	God's Money-Back Guarantee	99
36	Whatever You Think	101
37	Fruit Facts	103
38	Be Strong and Courageous!	105
39	You Can Overcome	108
40	The Cream of the Crop	111
41	Knowing God's Thoughts	113
42	Spirits Can't Die	115
43	The Book of Eternal Life	117
44	No Retirement Plan	120
45	How High Can You Jump?	122
46	Standing on the Waves	124
47	The World Needs You	126

48   Don't Quit. 129

49   I'm Going To. 131

50   Don't Be Afraid to Try 133

51   The Vine and the Branches. 136

52   The True Vine. 138

53   Freedom to Obey. 140

54   Whatever You Wish. 143

55   Potential Potency. 146

56   Your Triune Self. 149

57   Our Measure of Reality 152

58   Your Body Is Not Your True Self. 154

59   Your Body—God's Temple 157

60   The Soul's Potential. 160

61   Your Spirit's Potential. 162

62   Read the Instructions—the Bible. 165

63   Your Built-Ins Came Standard. 168

64   Greater Works Than Jesus 170

65   Your Godly Purpose 173

66   Do All You Can Dream. 175

67 Stop Worrying 178

68 Mind Control 181

69 Everyday Faith. 183

70 A Craving Desire 185

71 Follow the Narrow Road 188

72 Be One of the Few 191

73 The World View 193

74 The Third World 196

75 Buried Beneath. 198

76 Good for Something 201

77 Refuse to Be Satisfied 204

78 Nothing in Life Is Instant 207

79 Suppose. 210

80 Don't Be a Robber 213

81 From Out of God 216

82 The Inventor's Intention 219

83 What God Sees. 221

84 A New Battery 224

85 Bored and Tired 227

86	Back to Your Beginning 229
87	Your Creator's Demands and Commands . . 231
88	Dominate the Earth...................... 234
89	Always a Way Out 236
90	Move On............................... 238
91	Your Potential Is Limitless and Free........ 240
	About Dr. Myles Munroe................. 243

GOD,
THE SOURCE OF ALL

In the beginning was the Word, and the Word was with God, and the Word was God. He was with God in the beginning. All things were made through Him, and without Him nothing was made that was made. In Him was life… (John 1:1-4 NKJV).

The Bible tells us: "In the beginning, God…." That means before there was a beginning, there was God. Therefore, God began the beginning and verse 0 of the first chapter of Genesis might possibly read: In God was the beginning. Everything that is, was in God.

Everything that has ever been made was made by God. When we connect Genesis 1:0 and John 1:1, we see that the Word was with God in the beginning, not at the beginning.

Nothing that was created was made without the Word. In *the Word* was life. *Life* came out of God. Therefore, before you knew life, life was. *All* things were made by God. Everything you see, hear, smell, taste, and touch was in God before they came to be. Even what you discern first existed in God.

Now let me be a little ridiculous to prove my point. God had suns and clouds and planets in Him. The cows to make shoe leather, oil to run our cars, the ore from the mountains to make steel—all these things were in God. Everything on this earth is God's property. If God would ever call in His property, we would be in big trouble. All things were in God and belong to Him. God, in the beginning when there was nothing, contained everything that humans *have seen*. He also contained everything humans *will ever see*.

If you had talked to God on the highway of nothingness, you would have been talking to millions of cows and horses and mountains and trees and limousines and hotels and beaches. They all were in God, but no one saw them. God is omnipotent, always full of the potential to bring forth what you see. In essence, if you met God on the highway of nothing, by the corner of nowhere, before there was anything, and you shook His hand, you would be shaking hands with *everything*. You would *be* with potential.

***

God is with you—you are with Potential.

***

OMNIPOTENT GOD

Indeed My hand has laid the foundation of the earth,
and My right hand has stretched out the heavens;
when I call to them, they stand up together
(Isaiah 48:13 NKJV).

Everything in life was created with potential and possesses the potential principle. Creation abounds with potential because the Creator Himself is the potential principle. When we describe God, we often say He is omnipotent. Omnipotent means that God is always potent. Made up of two words: *omni,* meaning "always," and *potent,* meaning "full of power," *omnipotent* means that God is potentially everything. He has within Him the potential for all that is, was, or ever will be. He is omnipotent or omni-potent.

Everything that was, and everything that is, was in God. That's a very important concept. Everything that was and is, was in God. We have to start with God. Before God made anything, before He created things, there was only God. So before anything was, God is. God is the root, or Source, of all life.

Before there was time, time was—but it was in God. Before God created a galaxy or the Milky Way, they existed. Before there was a universe or a planetary system with the third planet called earth revolving around the sun—before any of that was—they were.

I wonder what it must have been like when God was just by Himself. Let's try to imagine that for a bit. Here's God. He steps out on nothing to view nothing, for there was nothing except God. And so God is standing on top of nothing, looking at nothing because everything was in Him.

**Created in His image, you
are potent with potential too.**

FROM NOTHINGNESS TO EVERYTHING

*By faith we understand that the universe was formed
at God's command, so that what is seen was not
made out of what was visible* (Hebrews 11:3).

In the beginning, God was pregnant with the universe and all things were made by Him. But how did these things come out of Him? How was the universe formed? All things were formed at God's command. He spat them out—poof! From the invisible came the visible. Things that are seen came from things that were unseen.

God always had everything in Him, but we couldn't see it. All we now see was once in an invisible state. Everything that man has ever seen first existed in an invisible state. (Please note that invisible does not mean nonexistent.)

All the buildings we see and the businesses we frequent—people making money and investing money—all that stuff began as ideas. We couldn't see them because they were in somebody's mind. The stores where we shop, also everything on the shelves and racks in those stores, began as ideas in someone's mind. They didn't exist before, yet they did. Although they weren't present in their current form, they existed as lumber and concrete and nails, cotton and wool and flax, steel and pulleys and motors.

In the beginning there was only God. At creation the entire unseen universe became visible. Everything that has been created was made by the word of God. Although it already existed, God spoke so that what was invisible could become visible. You would never have known it existed, except God spat it out in faith.

By faith God spat out what was in Him. Everything in Him started to come forth. What we now see was birthed by God from what was invisibly within Him. Whatever you see came from the unseen—nothing exists that was not at some time in God. Thus, *faith is not the evidence of things that do not exist. It is the evidence of things that are not yet seen*. Everything we see has always been. It became visible when God *spoke* it into being. God is the Source of life.

**Everything you see
has always been.**

THEN GOD SAID

Then God said… (Genesis 1:3,6,9,11,14,20,24,26,29).

What happened when God spoke at creation? How did He get the invisible to become visible? First let me broaden your idea of the word *spoke*.

Spoke was a process. What God spoke into visibility began as an idea in His mind. God first conceived in His mind what He wanted to create. He didn't just say, "I want this." The prophet Isaiah tells us that God created the earth by first planning its foundations (Isaiah 48:13). After the plans were in His mind, God spoke them into existence. When God was ready to speak, it was just a matter of taking what was in the plan and putting it on the site.

God laid the groundwork for the earth and spread out the heavens. He created the sun to shine during the day and the moon and stars at night. He gave every star a name. He ordered clouds to fill the sky and breezes to blow. He made the waves to roar in the sea. He sent rain to water the earth and grass to cover the hillside. Thunder and lightning were created by His command; hail and sleet were formed by His word. A wool-like blanket of snow He produced for winter; frost and dew He designed.

God was full of imagination. He was pregnant with many thoughts. His thoughts became ideas, and the ideas became images. Everything that is came out of God as He *spoke* those images. The unseen became seen—the invisible became visible.

For six days God created the heavens and the earth. On the seventh day He rested (Genesis 2:2-3). *Spoke* must be fairly serious. If God, who is almighty and all powerful, had to rest after creation, *spoke it* must have been very hard work.

When creation was completed, God rested. God was the first one to *sabbat*—He intended the Sabbath to be a blessing. He knows that life produces work, and work creates the need to rest.

Like God, you too are full of imagination.

A WORK
IN PROGRESS

*For we are God's handiwork, created in Christ Jesus
to do good works, which God prepared in advance
for us to do* (Ephesians 2:10).

The work of God is not complete—He has not delivered all His babies. He will keep on delivering as long as you deliver, because *you* are the continuation of His deliveries. God can still create. When you ask for something in prayer, God doesn't have to shift things around because He is going broke. If it doesn't exist in a visible form, God will speak it. He'll make whatever is necessary. He continues to be pregnant with much.

Because all things are in God, you can ask God for anything. An idea is around in God a long time before it comes out. Nothing we think or do is new (Ecclesiastes 1:9). Everything that has been done will be done again—what we think is new has already been here for a long time.

There's a guy in China right now who is thinking about the idea you thought was yours. When the idea came out of God, many people got it. Because everything comes out of God, you all received the idea from the same Source. Until that idea is transformed by action, God will continue to leak that idea into men and women. Why? Because God is a God of potential.

Although *He* is the Source of all things, He shares His omnipotent powers with His creation. We, like God, are pregnant with many things. We are full of imagination, having the potential power to be more than we visibly are. There are dreams, visions, plans and ideas in us that need to be released. God wants us to tap His power and use it, because *God made us with potential.*

Principles for discovering the hidden you: Everything that was and is, was in God. God is the Source of all potential. All things were formed at God's command so the invisible became visible. God planned the world in His mind before speaking it into existence.

You are the continuation
of God's deliveries.

MANY LOOK, FEW SEE

He took him outside and said, "Look up at the sky and count the stars—if indeed you can count them." Then he said to him, "So shall your offspring be" (Genesis 15:5).

A sculptor works in a very interesting way. I'm an artist of sorts, so I have a bit of an understanding how artists work. One thing I have learned is that you never argue with an artist until he is finished. Don't discuss anything with a painter or a sculptor until his work is completed. An artist can be very rude if you disturb him before he has accomplished what he intends to do, because he sees different from those who are not artists.

An artist can walk by the stone in your front yard and see a figure in it. He may stop by your house and beg you for a stone you have walked past many times without noticing. The dogs may have been doing stuff on it. You may even have been planning to get rid of it because it's a nuisance. But the artist walks into your yard and sees something beautiful in that stone beyond what you can imagine.

Two months later when the artist invites you to his workshop he says, "Do you see that? Do you know where that came from?"

"England or France?" you ask.

"No," says the artist. "It came from your yard."

"Do you mean…?"

"Yes."

"Five hundred dollars, please."

You were sitting on $500. The dogs were doing stuff on $500. But you couldn't see the potential in the rock.

There are many people who are being passed by because others don't see what is in them. But God has shown me what's in me, and I know it is in you too. My job is to stop you and say, "Can you see what's in you? Do you know your potential? Do you know that you are not just someone born in a ghetto over the hill? There's a wealth of potential in you."

Who you are is related to
where you came from.

GOD SEES THE AUTHENTIC YOU

So he asked Jesse, "Are these all the sons you have?"
"There is still the youngest," Jesse answered. "He is
tending the sheep." Samuel said, "Send for him; we
will not sit down until he arrives." Then the Lord
said, "Rise and anoint him; this is the one"
(1 Samuel 16:11-12).

They say Michelangelo used to walk around a block of marble for days—just walking around it, talking to himself. First he would see things in the rock; then he would go and take them out. Insight like that of a sculptor is seen in the Bible. When the world dumps and rejects you, and you land on the garbage heap of the world, God walks along and picks you up. He looks deep within you and sees a person of great worth.

Don't ever let anybody throw you away. You are not junk. When God looks at you, He sees things that everybody else ignores. You are worth so much that Jesus went to Calvary to salvage and reclaim you. The Spirit of God connected to your spirit is the only true judge of your worth. Don't accept the opinions of others because they do not see what God sees.

God looked at Adam and saw a world. He looked at Abraham and saw nations. In Jacob, a deceiver, He saw a Messiah. In Moses the murderer, God saw a deliverer. Can you imagine looking at a stammering young man and seeing the greatest leader in history? God saw a king in a shepherd boy. When the Israelites wanted a king, God sent Samuel to the home of Jesse. When Jesse heard why Samuel was there, he dressed up all his sons—the handsome one, the tall one, the curly-haired one, the strong one, the muscular one. All the sons of Jesse twirled out before Samuel, from the greatest to the least.

Finally, after Jesse had paraded all of his sons before him, Samuel said, "I'm sorry. None of these is God's choice for king. Do you have any other sons?" Jesse said, "Yes, well, but this guy's really smelly because he's been out with the sheep for some time." When Samuel saw David, the youngest, he said, "This is the one God wants."

When God looks at you,
He sees things that
everybody else ignores.

A WORTHWHILE
SOMEBODY

*Then God said, "Let Us make man in Our image,
according to Our likeness...." So God created man
in His own image, in the image of God He created
him; male and female He created them*
(Genesis 1:26-27 NKJV).

Were you the black sheep in your family? (You know God likes sheep.) Has your family told you that you are a nobody? Have you been put off and put out and told so many times that you will amount to nothing that you have begun to believe it? Do you *feel* like the black sheep?

You are probably the one God is waiting for in the house. God sees things deep within you that others can't see. They look at you and see a nobody; God looks at you and sees a worthwhile somebody.

You may spend your whole life competing with others—trying to prove that you are somebody—and still feel like nobody. Be free from that today! You do not have to live with that any longer. You don't have to *try* to be somebody, because you *are* somebody.

You will never discover who you were meant to be if you use another person to find yourself. You will never know what you can do by using what I've done to measure your ability. You will never know why you exist if you use my existence to measure it. All you will see is what I've done or who I am. If you want to know who you are, look at God. The key to understanding life is in the source of life, not in the life itself. You are who you are because God took you out of Himself. If you want to know who you are, you must look at the Creator, not the creation.

God created you by speaking to Himself. You came out of God and thus bear His image and likeness.

You contain the potential of your Source, God.

GOD SEES ALL

She gave this name to the Lord who spoke to her:
*"**You are the God who sees** me," for she said,*
*"I have now seen the One who **sees** me"*
(Genesis 16:13).

How you feel or what others say about you is not important. You are who God says you are; He sees in you more than you can possibly imagine. Your potential is limited only by God, not others.

God came to a frightened young man named Gideon. Gideon obviously thought God was talking to someone else when the angel of the Lord called him a mighty warrior (Judges 6:12). The angel didn't say, "Oh, coward. Do you know you have strength?" Nor did the angel say, "Oh black man, do you know that you can be like the white man?" The angel just came in and announced what he saw:

"Oh mighty man of war power." That means "Oh great warrior."

Think about it. Warrior? Gideon was hiding from the enemy trying to separate some wheat from the chaff so he wouldn't starve. He was doing it underground so no one could see him. When the angel said, "You are a brave man," Gideon started looking around to see who the angel was talking to.

God never tells us what others see. He never calls us what others call us. Gideon thought he was a coward. God knew him to be a great warrior and pronounced what He saw.

God also saw in Peter what others failed to see. His given name was Simon, which means *meek*. (Literally it means "unstable, flaky, leaf.") When Jesus met Simon, he was the flakiest, leafiest man you ever met. He was always going with the wind— changing his mind. But God saw a stone in the leaf. The first time Jesus met Peter, He changed Peter's name from Simon (leaf) to Peter (stone). Although Simon was an unstable guy, Jesus said, "I'm going to change your name. Your name is Peter." Peter acted like a leaf throughout Jesus' earthly ministry. Still Jesus called him *rock* every morning. Jesus saw in Peter something his mother had not seen. He kept chipping until finally, at Pentecost, Peter's true nature was revealed.

**Your potential is limited only
by God, not others.**

A GREAT TRAGEDY

*The land produced vegetation: plants bearing seed according to their kinds and trees **bearing fruit with seed in it according to their kinds**. And God saw that it was good* (Genesis 1:12).

One of the greatest tragedies in life is to watch human potential die untapped. Many potentially great men and women never realize their potential because they don't understand the nature and concept of the potential principle. *There's a wealth of potential in you.* My purpose is to help you understand that potential and then release it for the benefit of others, and yourself. You must decide if you are going to rob the world or bless it with the rich, valuable, potent, untapped resources locked away within you.

As I walk the streets of our cities, my heart frequently weeps as I encounter and observe the wasted, broken, disoriented lives of individuals who, years before, were talented, intelligent, aspiring high-school classmates. During their youth they had dreams, desires, plans and aspirations.

Today they are lost in a maze of substance abuse, alcoholism, purposelessness and poorly chosen friends. Their lives are aimless, their decisions haphazard. This enormous tragedy saddens me. *What could have been* has become *what should have been.* The *wealth of dreams* has been dashed into the *poverty of discouragement.*

Everything in life was created with potential and possesses the potential principle. In every seed there is a tree...in every bird a flock...in every fish a school...in every sheep a flock...in every cow a herd...in every boy a man...in every girl a woman... in every nation a generation. Tragedy strikes when a tree dies in a seed, a man in a boy, a woman in a girl, an idea in a mind. For untold millions, visions die unseen, songs die unsung, plans die unexecuted and futures die buried in the past. The problems of our world go unanswered because potential remains buried.

God created everything with potential, including you. He placed the seed of each thing within itself, and planted within each person or thing He created the ability to be much more than it is at any one moment. Thus, everything in life has potential.

You must decide if you are going to rob the world or bless it.

WHAT GOD SEES IN YOU

Indeed, the very hairs of your head are all numbered.
*Don't be afraid; you are **worth more** than*
many sparrows (Luke 12:7).

I wonder what God sees as He walks around you. I'm sure He sees beautiful things in you, but you are believing what other people are saying. People say: "You are no good. You'll never be somebody." But God is saying: "I see a jewel." We are diamonds in the rough. Just keep on believing that. Keep on moving forward to your goal. Remember that there is something in you more precious than what others have said about you. The sculptor never gives up until he gets out of the rock what he sees.

I have a sculpture in my home that isn't what I intended it to be because as I was chiseling, part of it was knocked off by too much pressure. Consequently, I could no longer create the image I had intended. So I walked around it thinking, "I've gotta change my concept a little." I had to rethink how to retain the beauty of the sculpture though I had lost an important part of the wood.

Eventually, I modified my design. But I am the only person who knows that. People have admired that piece of wood saying, "Wow! This is beautiful." And I never tell them that what they see is not what they were originally supposed to see.

That piece of sculpture sitting in my home reminds me of your life and mine. Parts of our lives have been knocked off by our past. We've done some dumb things that have messed up the beauty God intended. But look what God has done. He's saved us. Instead of discarding us because we have not turned out like He intended us to be, He has taken us—including our marred and chipped and rusted and knocked-off past—and formed us into something beautiful.

When people look at you and think you are the best thing that ever came down the pike, don't tell them what you used to be. Just say, "Thank you very much. The Chief Sculptor had His hands on me."

**God can bring beauty
out of your mistakes.**

CHRIST IN YOU

To them God has chosen to make known among the Gentiles the glorious riches of this mystery, which is Christ in you, the hope of glory (Colossians 1:27).

I wonder what God sees when He looks at you. I believe He sees Christ. When God looks at you, He does not see you. He sees Christ. Paul, when writing to the Colossian church, proclaimed that God had chosen to make known a mystery. *What God sees when He looks at you is Christ.*

Most of us want to be like Jesus. That's not what God wants. God wants us to be like Christ. Jesus came to show us what Christ looks like when He takes on human form. But it is Christ that God's looking at. God sees Christ in you. That's the hope of glory—*Christ in you*. Let me explain.

Christ is the image of God. The word *image* does not mean "a statue of something." It means "the essence of the being." That means when God created you, He created you in His image, and His image is Christ. That's why the Bible never calls us the Body of Jesus. Jesus was the human manifestation of the heavenly Christ. We humans on earth, with all our fallibilities and weaknesses—God pronounces on us: "You are the body of Christ."

If we go to God and say, "God, please introduce me to Your people," God will say, "Sure. Here is Christ." But we'll say, "No. No. No. I want to meet Christ," to which God will reply, "Sure. Here's Christ" as He shows us the Church. When we want to meet Christ, God will show us the Church. But we can't accept this because we think Christ is in Heaven. No, He isn't. *Jesus* is in Heaven. *Christ* is sitting in your clothes, living in the body of the believer. Christ is the essence of God—He's God Himself.

Although you may say, "I want to be like Jesus," God says, "There's something deeper." You were lost and Jesus came to bring you back. God sent Jesus so you could see yourself.

When you want to meet Christ, God will show you the Church.

THE
ADVERSARY

*The reason the Son of God appeared was to
destroy the devil's work* (1 John 3:8).

Satan came into our lives to minimize, nullify,
and destroy our potential. He has killed, stolen,
and destroyed what God planted deep within each
person. Through the years, the devil has succeeded
in convincing men and women, each with a little
part of God, that they are worthless, rotten, incapa-
ble people. But in the fullness of time Jesus came
into the world to address this very problem.

There are two destroyers in the world. One is
satan; the other is Jesus. Satan comes to destroy,
and Jesus comes to destroy. Satan is God's enemy
and ours. He is our adversary, out to blind us to the
truth of God's love and the wisdom that offers us

hope. He is a destruction mechanism that comes to destroy, kill and steal. What is he destroying? First satan destroyed humankind's potential to be like our Creator. Satan said, "Do you want to be like God? Pick that fruit." The man and woman already were like God, but by following satan's advice they were destroyed. Their potential to be like God was clogged up right then—it was capped off.

Satan continued to work his art of deception when he said, "God is hiding something from you." He destroyed Adam and Eve's concept of God. God became Someone who was holding back on them. Satan said, "God doesn't want you to know what He knows." Adam and Eve were *born* related in spirit with God. God *created* them to know Him. Yet, satan stole both humankind's potential to be like God and our understanding of God.

Principles for discovering the hidden you: All things have the same components and essence as their source. When God created human beings, He spoke to Himself. You will never know yourself by relating to the creation, only to the Creator. Your potential is much greater than what you are right now. Your potential is limited only by God, not others. God sees Christ in you.

Jesus came to destroy
the works of the devil.

14

THE LIAR

*…the devil…was a murderer from the beginning,
not holding to the truth, for there is no truth in him.
When he lies, he speaks his native language, for he is
a liar and the father of lies* (John 8:44).

The deceiver also distorted man's self-concept. He said to them: "Look at you. You are naked." So the man and woman felt bad about themselves and they put on clothes. They tried to cover up their bodies.

Ever since that day, we have become professional *"cover-ups."* We don't like ourselves. We don't like our physical bodies. Yuk! I don't like how skinny I am…how fat I am…how my hair grows…how my eyes are…how my lips are. I don't like my black, brown, red, yellow, or white skin. So we try to cover up what we don't like. It is strange how we work on things. If our hair is curly, we straighten it. If our skin is too pale, we get a tan. We don't like what we are. Nobody is satisfied with themselves. We all walk around saying, "Why do you want to be like me? I want to be like you."

We have become professional "cover-ups." This attitude is from the devil. We can't just be ourselves because satan has destroyed our appreciation of what God made. Our potential has been distorted so that we don't want to be black or tall or fat. We don't want to have curly hair or fat lips or small eyes. We have accepted satan's ploy to destroy our esteem for the beautiful creation God made us to be.

Satan, who comes to destroy everything God created, has destroyed our concepts of ourselves. Because we do not like ourselves, we do all kinds of dumb things. If you love yourself, you are not going to lower your standards. You will not sell yourself to anybody. You won't allow anybody to buy you—you are too expensive.

Satan destroyed man's true intelligence, which is a spiritual relationship with God. When we are connected with God, our spirits can know anything. That's why the knowledge God communicates is not learned. It is discerned. Your real intelligence is not studied; it is discerned. Wow!

The knowledge of God isn't found in any book; it's a deeper knowledge.

ABUNDANT LIFE

*[Jesus said] ...I have come that they may have life,
and that they may have it more abundantly*
(John 10:10 NKJV).

When humans lost their relationship with God, they became victims of education. We began to look to books and movies and the words of others—what we can see, hear, taste, feel, and touch—to gain knowledge. Those things became our sources of information. When satan destroyed our real intelligence, we looked outside ourselves to find knowledge.

By destroying our relationship with God, satan capped off our life potential. The devil continually tries to destroy any possibility that we might become more than we already are. Satan chops up your self-confidence and slams the door on your potential by convincing you that you are nothing:

"You'll never rise above your family's status. You'll never go beyond where your neighborhood took you. You'll never be any more than your mom and your dad. You don't stand a chance." The devil has been teaching and preaching that to keep us down. He is very skilled at this deceptive art.

But Jesus came to destroy satan's lies. He came to free us from those things that retard, distort, and short-circuit everything we are capable of being and doing.

We think life is what we have now. No! In the Greek, the same word is used for *abundance* as is used for *fountain*. Jesus came to take the cap off your well…to unclog the true you…to open the capacity of who you are and who you can be.

Jesus didn't come just to take off your well cover. He came to start an explosion of water—a potential welling up and never stopping. Jesus said, *"Whoever believes in me, as Scripture has said, rivers of living water will flow from within them"* (John 7:38). Jesus also said, *"whoever drinks the water I give them will never thirst. Indeed, the water I give them will become in them a spring of water welling up to eternal life"* (John 4:14).

Jesus came so we can have fountains of life. Wow, that's impressive to me!

Jesus came to
destroy satan's lies.

STRONGHOLDS

*The weapons we fight with are not the weapons of the world. On the contrary, they have divine power to demolish **strongholds*** (2 Corinthians 10:4).

Until we get saved, we don't have life. If you became born again recently, you are finally getting back to your real self. All you have done for the past ten or twenty years that made you think you were somebody is but a trickle. You haven't changed the world. You haven't changed someone's life for eternity yet. You haven't touched a youngster for eternal life yet. You may have put clothes on homeless people's backs, but you haven't put anything on their spirits. You haven't done anything yet! But there is a fountain, an abundance of life, welling up in you so you can do and be. It begins when you return to your Source through Jesus Christ.

Are there things in your life that have been holding you back from the things you should be doing? Are you a potential leader in your community but you're full of alcohol and you're lying in the gutter? Has cocaine stolen your potential to be the top student in your class? Is your brain all messed up so you can't even think any more? Are you in danger of being kicked out of school though you were an A student before you took the stuff? Have you run off with a dumb guy and gotten pregnant? Do you have to drop out of school and give up your visions of becoming a doctor or a lawyer, scientist, or agricultural expert? Has sin clogged up your potential?

Sin clogs our potential. It messes up the plan God has for each of our lives. It takes away the "And they lived happily ever after" and replaces it with "And they struggled but didn't make it through the day." Don't let that be the last chapter in the book God has written on you. God sent Jesus to die for you, not for Himself. The problem is that *you* don't know *your* potential. You have been destroyed by the devil, and sin is stunting your growth.

Sin clogs up your potential. It messes up the plan God has for your life.

WISDOM AND YOU

So where does this leave the philosophers, the scholars, and the world's brilliant debaters? God has made the wisdom of this world look foolish. Since God in his wisdom saw to it that the world would never know him through human wisdom, he has used our foolish preaching to save those who believe. It is foolish to the Jews, who ask for signs from heaven. And it is foolish to the Greeks, who seek human wisdom (1 Corinthians 1:20-22 New Living Translation).

Potential is everything that a thing is, that has not yet been seen or manifested. Everything in life begins as potential. All things have the potential to fulfill themselves, because God created everything with potential. There is no fulfillment in life without understanding the reason for being. If we want to know the real potential of something, we first have to know what that thing was created to do.

So if you have a seed in your hand, a kernel of corn or a pea, you will never get the seed's complete fulfillment until you know that there is a plant inside that seed. It is only as we look beyond the seed to the plant that we understand its true potential. God created each person with a great wealth of potential.

The most important thing for you and me, as human beings, is to try and find out for the rest of our lives what is the purpose for everything in life. That is our main goal. Unless we ask ourselves, "What is the purpose for everything in life?" we will die without having experienced the potential of everything. We will miss the wisdom of God in creation.

Did you know that satan still has wisdom? Ezekiel 28:17 tells us that satan's wisdom became corrupted. God could not take back what He had given, so satan is still wise. But his wisdom is corrupt. God is the Creator, but satan is the perverter. God creates everything; satan creates nothing. But everything God creates, satan perverts.

God created each person with a great wealth of potential.

PERVERSIONS

*And don't forget Sodom and Gomorrah and
their neighboring towns, which were filled with
immorality and every kind of sexual **perversion**.
Those cities were destroyed by fire and serve as a
warning of the eternal fire of God's judgment*
(Jude 1:7 NLT).

Before the fall, lucifer's responsibility in Heaven was to be the music and worship leader. He was designed with the potential not only to lead in music and worship, but also to produce it. As soon as he started fanning his wings, the angels started singing. He had the potential to lead all Heaven in worship and music. That's why music is such an important part of our world today. Satan uses a huge amount of money to support today's music industry—hundreds of millions every year. And the Church can't raise even one million.

But God still has the final word. God put music into the Church and into us. He calls for us to praise Him. Satan's potential is related to his purpose. God considers foolishness any wisdom that does not fulfill its original purpose.

If you are a very skillful musician, but you use it to create lewdness and sensuality, and to cause people to go into perversion, then God calls that foolishness. For when you use the belief God has given to you to say you don't believe in Him, your wisdom becomes foolishness. The fool says in his heart, "There is no God." He takes the ability God gave him to believe and uses that belief power to not believe in God. God says, "That's foolishness!" (1 Corinthians 1:20-22).

But for those who believe in Jesus Christ, God's apparent foolishness is revealed as true wisdom. The wisest of human thoughts appears puny beside this foolishness of God, and the greatest of man's strengths pales beside Christ's weakness. What is a stumbling block or pure foolishness for those who don't believe in Christ stands, for the Christian, as a towering source of truth, strength and hope. *That* is wisdom.

God considers it foolishness
any wisdom that does not
fulfill its original purpose.

GOD'S SECRET WISDOM

We do, however, speak a message of wisdom among the mature, but not the wisdom of this age or of the rulers of this age, who are coming to nothing. No, **we speak of God's secret wisdom**, *a wisdom that has been hidden and that God destined for our glory before time began* (1 Corinthians 2:6-7).

Before you were born, God placed in you a secret wisdom. He planted within you a potential something—a wisdom to know who you are and what you were created to be and do. That potential something was in God, but He allowed it to leak into you when He pulled you out of Himself. It's a hidden understanding that follows neither the wisdom of our society nor the insights of our leaders. Unlike the wisdom of the world, which is worthless, God's secret wisdom about you is a priceless jewel.

Many people die without unveiling their wealth of wisdom. They die in total foolishness, without experiencing the life that dwells within. What a pity! They have missed God's secret wisdom. *Secret* here does not mean "to be withheld from." It rather has the meaning of "to have never known existed." There is a difference. God is not holding back from the world. He is not withholding from us our true potential. It's just that we have never known that it is within us. They have missed the wisdom God designed before the beginning of time for the honor of humankind.

It's a secret wisdom from God that He is keeping for us. It was in God and now it dwells in *us*. I know you may find that hard to accept—perhaps you think I am a mad man. But the truth is you'll be shocked when you understand who you really are. You don't know what you have inside that you are selling so cheaply. You have God's secret wisdom, a wisdom that you should be using to discover His destiny for you.

You were born with secret wisdom that came right out of God.

BUT...

*That is what the Scriptures mean when they say,
"No eye has seen, no ear has heard, and no mind has
imagined what God has prepared for those who love
him." But it was to us that God revealed these
things by his Spirit. For his Spirit searches out
everything and shows us God's deep secrets*
(1 Corinthians 2:9-10 NLT).

*But it was to us that God has revealed these things by
His Spirit."* The word *but* indicates a change. But
inserts hope in the midst of hopelessness. Most people do not know what God intends for their lives.
They have not seen their secret wisdom, nor have
they heard about it. They have never even thought
about it because there are certain things we cannot
understand unless the Holy Spirit reveals them to
us. They are so deep within our potential that we
need help to drag them out.

God had those deep things within Him before He made us; He put them into us at birth. But we don't know they exist because sin has clogged up the entryway. It is as if God struck a well and put wealth in it. Wealth is in you—in your personality, in your being. But it has been clogged up and capped off by sin.

When you were born, the cap over your potential was firmly in place. Outside God's grace you will never know what is buried beneath. Billions of dollars of wealth are buried within you, but you are not aware of it. You walk along, but you don't know who you are. You don't understand that what you see is merely the shadow of your potential. That's why the Bible says, *"nor have entered into the heart of man the things God has prepared for those who love Him"* (1 Corinthians 2:9 NKJV). Wow!

In His mercy, God has placed within each of us the answer to every dilemma. After the resurrection of Jesus Christ, God sent the gift of the Holy Spirit. That same Spirit, which we receive at our new birth, provides the connection between our spirits and God's secret wisdom.

But...

God's Spirit searches out everything and shows us His deep secrets that lead to wisdom.

BORN OF THE SPIRIT

Jesus answered, "Very truly I tell you, no one can enter the kingdom of God unless they are born of water and the Spirit" (John 3:5).

Have you ever wondered why we have to be born of the Spirit? Why does the Holy Spirit connect with our spirits? Think for a moment about your spirit. The deepest knowledge about ourselves comes to us through our spirits—we can't know anything deeper than our spirits reveal. No one knows more about you than you know about yourself, for who can understand someone better than their own spirit (1 Corinthians 2:11)?

Before your new birth in Christ, you were spiritually dead. Your spirit was paralyzed for 15, 20, or 30 years (however long it took you to get saved). You can't truly know yourself until you become spiritually alive.

If you are not a Christian, you don't really know who you are. Only people's spirits know the real thoughts of what they are supposed to be. We will never know who we are supposed to be until we accept Jesus as our Savior and receive God's gift of His Spirit.

If then, your spirit doesn't know any more about you than what it has learned since you got saved, look at how little it knows. Just look at you. Do you know where you would be if you had not been saved? Now don't get me wrong. You aren't perfect yet. Don't get carried away. You know there is still much that needs to be worked on—many things that need to be refined.

But do you know what happens? The more we know about who we are, the more our attitude toward ourselves changes. Isn't that something! The minute we realize who we are we say, "Wait a minute. Now I'm a child of God," so we start changing our language and our habits. We think, "Gosh, I'm a prosperous person," and we start expecting good things to happen in our lives. As our knowledge about who we are grows, our lives change for the better.

The Holy Spirit within you goes straight for the things that are clogging you up and dragging you down.

HOLY SPIRIT DEEP DIVE

*The words of the mouth are deep waters, but
the fountain of wisdom is a rushing stream*
(Proverbs 18:4).

The Holy Spirit is the bucket that allows us to understand the wisdom and intentions of our hearts. God has prepared so many deep things about who we are. Our eyes can't see them, nor can our minds conceive them, yet God is revealing them to us through His Spirit. God doesn't want us to wait until Heaven to know our full potential. He didn't give birth to us so we can develop our potential in Heaven. (In fact, in Heaven we will already have finished maximizing our potential.) God wants us to realize here on this planet who we are. Only the Holy Spirit searches "the deep things of God."

You may have received the revelation of what it cost God to love you. Others have not. You may be ready to walk into a deeper level of knowledge; others are not. God beckons you to take another step into a deeper, more relevant knowledge of your potential in Christ—though you may have been saved for years. You need to take this step because you still don't know who you are. Only the Holy Spirit can reveal this truth to you. You cannot perceive your true potential unless the Holy Spirit gives it to your eyes and ears and mind.

It's the Holy Spirit's job to search out the deep things of God and interpret them so we can understand them. Now, listen. Trying to figure out God Himself is deep. Our efforts to understand God could take a million years or more. How can we possibly understand God's deep things—the great mysteries He has to share with us? Can we imagine that the Source of the deep things of God might be connected to us? Can we go inside God to those things that are deep within Him?

Yes, we can! God has given us His Spirit so we can understand all the things He oozed into us.

**You cannot perceive your
true potential unless the
Holy Spirit reveals it to you.**

THERE IS MORE

We have not received the spirit of the world but the
Spirit who is from God, that we may understand
what God has freely given us (1 Corinthians 2:12).

I'm hooked on those little things that are leaking out in me—His revelations. I'm glad the Holy Spirit can go deep to show me those things about you and me that God knows and wants to share. That's mind-blowing!

There are things about you, concerning who you can be, that you haven't discovered yet—holy things that only the Holy Spirit can explain. God reveals His deep things to you through the Holy Spirit because He knows you would not believe them if they were simply told to you through your mind. Your mind cannot possibly comprehend all that God has prepared for you to be.

Forget what others have told you about who you can be. That's a joke. Don't even consider it. That is not all you can be, because the deepest things you can know about yourself are not in your mind or your emotions or even in your body. They are in your spirit. The deepest things you can know about yourself are what you get from your spirit. You'll never be fulfilled without God, because you are looking for what God has.

That's why God gives you the Holy Spirit. The Spirit goes deep inside you to capture the wealth of your potential. He pulls deep from within you the answers to your spirit's cries, showing you who you are and why He created you. You will never be fulfilled until you understand why God made you. You will only walk around confused, thinking, "There's gotta be more. There's gotta be more."

And there is!

The deepest things you can know about yourself are in your spirit.

GOD'S BUCKET
OF HOPE

But God has revealed them to us through His Spirit.
For the Spirit searches all things, yes, the deep
things of God (1 Corinthians 2:10 NKJV).

Do you want to know how cute you can be? Check God out. Do you want to know how smart you are? Go back to God. Your potential is buried in God. We think going to the moon is great—we should see what God had planned that we didn't follow. Our eyes will never see the stuff God prepared for us, nor will our ears hear it. Only the Holy Spirit can reveal to us the deep things of God that tell us who we are.

Through the gift of the Holy Spirit, you can reestablish your relationship with God. The Holy Spirit, connected with your spirit, unravels the knots that have bound your thoughts, removes the streaks that have blurred your vision and clears the debris that has hidden your potential. Working like a sculptor, He brings out the beauty hidden deep within your being, because that is the real you.

Open your life to Jesus Christ. Allow God to reveal His secret wisdom concerning you. See with your eyes and hear with your ears things you have never seen or heard before. Conceive with your mind thoughts that have never occurred to you. Cooperate with the Holy Spirit as He sucks out of God and into you the depths of the riches God prepared for you. Live the rest of your life building an atmosphere where it is possible for the Holy Spirit to use you as He takes His bucket of hope, dips it deep into the wells of your potential, and pulls it to the top of your senses.

Principles for discovering the hidden you: The potential for everything is related to its purpose for being. The wisdom of the world is a foolish, corrupt wisdom. For believers, Jesus Christ is both the power and the wisdom of God. God placed wisdom in you before you were born. You will never know who you are supposed to be until you accept Jesus as your Savior and receive the gift of God's Spirit.

Drink deeply, growing in the knowledge of who you really are in God. That's my dream for you.

FEELIN' GOOD

*You have searched me, Lord, and you know me.
You know when I sit and when I rise; you perceive
my thoughts from afar. ...Such knowledge is too
wonderful for me... For you created my inmost
being; you knit me together in my mother's womb.
I praise you because I am fearfully and wonderfully
made...* (Psalm 139:1-2,6,13-14).

If you feel good about yourself, you will feel good about other people. In other words, only after you see yourself as a worthwhile person can you appreciate others as worthwhile people. That's a very important insight because many people do not feel good about themselves. They look at themselves and wonder why God made them; or they doubt that anyone can find any good in them. But remember, God sees what others, and we ourselves, can't see. God looks at us and sees that we are worth feeling good about. We are special to God. We are valuable and important.

The crowning work of creation came on the sixth day when God created human beings. As He looked around Him, God pronounced His creation to be good. That includes you! God looked at the man and the woman He had made and declared them to be "very good." God has a good attitude toward you. He created you in His image and drew you out of Himself. Before you were born, you were in God. Part of His potential has been placed within you.

Before the beginning was, God is (Genesis 1:0). God is so big He began the beginning. There could not be a beginning without God, because God got start started. Before start started, however, God had a finished plan for your life. Your potential is not a trial-and-error experience.

Psalm 139 tells us that God planned each of your days before you were even born. Before you were formed, God knew you. He took great care in creating you. No part of your being was made without God's knowledge and careful concern. God wants each of us. He gives us what no other part of His creation received: His breath of life (Genesis 2:7).

God designed and predetermined
you to be a success story.

NO MISTAKES

In Him also we have obtained an inheritance, being predestined according to the purpose of Him who works all things according to the counsel of His will (Ephesians 1:11 NKJV).

Have you ever felt like you were a mistake? Have your parents told you they wished you had never been born? You may have come into this world as the result of a rape. But the fact that you were conceived is more important than how you were conceived. Some people go around dealing only with *how* things happened—but God is concerned with *the fact* that He allowed your conception to happen.

You may have been conceived out of wedlock. Being omnipotent, God had the power to prevent your conception. Yet God allowed it because He wanted you to show up. You are here because God wanted you to be born. How you came isn't important. What matters is that you are here. And if you are here, God created you with care (Psalm 139:13).

King David doesn't describe your mother in Psalm 139—she may have been an alcoholic or a drug addict, or a prostitute. He is concerned with *you*. He describes how God knit you together in your mother's womb without describing what that womb was like. The womb in which you were knit together is no longer important. *You* are important. Your very existence means God wants you to exist. You are somebody special, simply because you were born.

My frame was not hidden from you when I was made in the secret place, when I was woven together in the depths of the earth. Your eyes saw my unformed body... (Psalm 139:15-16).

God saw you in your mother's womb when you were a tiny baby—a one-centimeter embryo. He looked into the secret place in your mother's womb and saw you. From the second were conceived, God tenderly created you and watched you grow. God planned for you to be born.

You are here because God wanted you to be born.

YOUR BOOK'S SEQUEL

All the days ordained for me were written in Your
book before one of them came to be (Psalm 139:16).

God designed you to be somebody. He looked at your unformed body and declared, "This child is good." All His plans for your life were set out long before you took a breath. He wrote out the order of your days before you lived even one day (Psalm 139:16). There's a book about you. Some chapters God wrote about you haven't even been touched yet.

You may be playing around in the Index or you have spent years in the Table of Contents. Perhaps you are 30 years old and you still don't know God's plan for your life. That's playing around on the contents page. You are 30 years old and still wondering what you are supposed to be. You haven't even started yet. Others have jumped ahead of God's plan. Though His design calls for you to be married in Chapter 17, you got married in Chapter 2.

You may have ignored the things God wanted you to learn and experience in Chapters 2 through 16 so you would be prepared for marriage in Chapter 17. The plan He wrote for you is perfect and right. No detail or part is missing. You have the potential to live out all that God has planned for your life— but only if you accept Jesus Christ as your Savior and Lord. That's the first step toward understanding why you were born.

Though you may have messed up God's perfect plan for your life, He graciously offers to write another book for you. He puts you back in Chapter 1 so you can live the many details of His plan. That's what being born again is all about. It's the opportunity to start over—it's finally getting back to the first chapter of God's book on you. Self-acceptance is the key to healthy self-esteem. Accept yourself as God made you. Allow His power to transform your weakness.

God offers you a rewrite, a do-over.

TO HIM
BE GLORY

*Now to him who is able to do immeasurably
more than all we ask or imagine, according to his
power that is at work within us, to him be glory
in the church and in Christ Jesus throughout all
generations, for ever and ever! Amen*
(Ephesians 3:20-21).

Not only did God carefully plan for the details
of your life, He also determined how your life
would fit into His total plan for humanity. Part of
the answer to the why of our birth is revealed in
God's desire that we should show forth His glory.
The glory of God is the excess of His nature. It's all
the potential of our omnipotent God that has not yet
been revealed. He's full of so much more than we
can think or imagine and He's waiting to use us to
realize that potential.

Throughout the Bible, God tells us to make His name great in the earth. Praise and thanks are due God's name, which is great and awesome (Psalm 44:8, 99:3). His name is to be proclaimed among the nations (Malachi 1:11) as well as in Israel (Psalm 76:1). His name is holy (Luke 1:49; Psalm 99:3) and mighty in power (Jeremiah 10:6). Everything is done for "His name's sake." To understand this concept, we must also understand that the Hebrew concept of "name" literally is synonymous with the object. In other words, the name of the thing *is* the thing. Therefore, the name of God is Himself, and He is His name. To glorify His name, then, means exposing His nature.

God created *you* to bring glory to His name. His predestined plan for *your* life was designed to bring Him glory. He knows there is more to you than we can see because He placed part of Himself in you. His plan for your life is part of His creative work— through you God wants to continue the birth of His potential. Because you share God's omnipotent nature, Jesus said you can do even greater things than He did, if you only believe (Mark 11:23).

Your life was designed to bring Him glory.

JUST BELIEVE, DUMMY!

Jesus looked at them and said, "With man this is impossible, but not with God; all things are possible with God" (Mark 10:27).

Mark chapter 11 is all about if you can believe what you desire hard enough, God says it will be done. God gives us a little glimpse into our potential. It's as though God looks at the ideas He stored in us and says with a voice of disappointment, "If you only knew what you can do." That's the attitude of God toward you and me. God is totally disappointed in us because He knows what we can do. But we don't. And so He says to us, "All things are possible if you'd just believe, dummy." He's always knocking the limits off our lives.

Too often we are not willing to *believe* like God defines believe. God does not say, "Everything is possible if you get the idea." Things don't become reality because we have an idea. We have to believe in the idea and commit ourselves to it—abandoning ourselves to it—even if it costs us our lives. That's what it takes to believe in the Lord Jesus Christ—to lose our lives, to abandon ourselves. We must say, "I'm going to go into eternity believing in Jesus. I'm not sure what's out there, but I'm going to ride on that Name and that atonement."

God isn't impressed by your dreams. It's easier to dream an idea than to work it out. Thinking is great. But all things are possible when we *believe*. Jesus says in Mark 11:24, *"Whatever you ask for in prayer, **believe** that you have received it, and it will be yours."* God's work in creation began with a plan. God conceived in His mind what He wanted before speaking His creations into visible form. By the time God was ready to speak, it was just a matter of taking what was in the plan and putting it on the site.

Everything is possible if you abandon yourself to an idea for which you are willing to lose your life.

FIRST A THOUGHT

*He who forms the mountains, who creates the wind,
and **who reveals his thoughts** to mankind, who
turns dawn to darkness, and treads on the heights
of the earth—the Lord God Almighty is his name*
(Amos 4:13).

A *thought* is a silent word, so a *word* is an exposed thought. Everything in life starts in the thought form—it's a thought first. After it's said, it is no longer a thought. It becomes a word.

The next step is an *idea.* An idea is the concept of the thought—it has moved into a reality. Ideas are potentials.

The third level of operation is what I call *imagination.* Imagination changes an idea into a plan. If you have an idea it can come and go. You have many ideas in a day—what to cook, what to wear, what to do. You may decide the night before what you are going to wear in the morning and then wake up with a different idea. Ideas change. But if an idea develops into an imagination, it means the idea has become a plan. It is still not written or drawn, but it is in your head. Imagination is therefore a plan that is not documented. It is a visual display of your thoughts and ideas. Ephesians 3:20 challenges us to believe God is able and willing to do *"exceeding abundantly far beyond all we can think or imagine."* He dares us to use our imaginations.

If you want to be successful in life, take your ideas and turn them into imagination; then take imagination and duplicate it physically. Put it down. Let it become a plan of action.

Many people never get beyond the idea stage. That's sad. They are usually followers. The people who get to the imagination stage often talk a lot, but do nothing. They are dreamers.

But when people take their imagination, put it on paper, and take action, you are looking at visionaries becoming missionaries. Visionaries see great things in their minds, but their visions never make it to mission. When a visionary becomes a missionary, you have people who are going to change the world!

**Turn your thoughts
into actions.**

PLANS AND GOALS

*"For I know **the plans I have for you**," declares the Lord, "**plans to prosper** you and not to harm you, **plans to give you hope and a future"***
(Jeremiah 29:11).

God wants us to become people who have plans. He says, "Use your imagination. I won't give you a thought if you can't do it. If you think it, I'm ready to do it." Plans are documented imaginations. If you can document an imagination, you've developed a plan for action.

If you are having problems in your life, I mean real problems, you probably don't have a piece of paper on which you have documented your plans for the next five years. If there is no goal in front of you, you'll fall into the hazardous holes behind you. If there is no vision in front of you to pull you on, you will be dragged back to the path you know well. If your imagination is not documented, it will soon ferment into vapor and disillusionment.

Let me explain. If you don't have on paper a general plan for your life, you may decide something one minute only to change it five minutes later. You will be confused, disoriented, misguided, and frustrated. Ideas must be put down if they are to influence the way you live.

Many of us plan our meals for the next week, but we have nothing planned for our lives. The food we eat just goes away—it doesn't touch the future. Stop. Set your course. Imagine into your future as far as you can. Chart what you are going to do for the next five weeks, five months, five years. Start imagining what you want to be, what you want to accomplish, where you want to go, who you want to influence. Write it down then put it in a convenient location so you can check your progress, seeing how close you are to your next goal.

You will be amazed how that will encourage you. You will begin to see God's power at work within you. Don't worry how you are going to meet all your goals. God says, "You make the plan and I will give the answer how it will be accomplished."

**Progress requires
a plan of action.**

DESTINED BY GOD

I can do all things through Christ who strengthens me (Philippians 4:13 NKJV).

God created you to change the world. He carefully designed a plan for your life that allows you to share in His work of creation. Because you were made in God's image, you share His potential to be and do much more than is visible now. Everything you see was originally a thought in the mind of God—an invisible idea that God worked into sight. Make a plan. Give yourself something to be motivated toward. As you dream, think, imagine, and plan who you want to be, you will begin to see why God created you and the work He has designed you to do. You are destined by God to reveal His glory—His very nature.

When looking back over his years in the Lord's service, the apostle Paul stated he could do all things through Christ who strengthens him. The Greek terminology for *strengthen* does not mean we are weak and God comes and props us up. Paul is saying, "I can do all things through the potential of Christ who infuses me with the ability to do all things." This strength is a continual ability infused into us because we are connected to Christ. Thus our potential is not limited to doing *some* of the things God asks us to do. We can do *all things* because the ability to do so is already deposited in us. The basis for this deposit of Christ's ability goes back to God's work in creation.

Principles for discovering the hidden you: You are worth feeling good about because God wanted you to be born. God has a detailed plan for your life. The first step in living out God's plan is accepting Jesus Christ as your Savior and Lord. God created you with a part of His potential so you could expose and share in His glory. God's glory is the excess of His potential—His many plans that wait to be revealed through you. Develop a plan for your life that fulfills some of the possibilities God placed within you before you were born. Then believe and work them into existence.

**Believe you can do
all things through Christ.**

33

NOTHING NAMED "CAN'T"

*He gives **strength** to the weary and increases the power of the weak* (Isaiah 40:29).

For about two years my little boy has been coming to me when he's trying to do something and saying, "I can't do this." I always respond to him by saying, "There is nothing named 'can't.'" When he comes back to me and says, "I don't know how to do it," I always reply, "There's always a way to do everything."

One time my son and I were out in the yard playing bat and ball. I was throwing the ball to him and he kept on missing with the bat. Finally he became really upset and said, "I can't do that," to which I replied, "There's nothing named 'can't.'" Slowly he repeated after me, "There's nothing named 'can't.'"

Then I said, "Hold the bat," and I threw the ball. He hit the ball and then said, "There's nothing named 'can't.'"

Several days later when I stopped by home to drop off my daughter, my son came running and wanted to play basketball. When I said that I had to go back to the office to do some work, he insisted that he wanted to play ball with me then. When I again replied that I *had* to go to the office, he said, "There's nothing named 'can't.'"

Do you see the point? If he begins to think that way at four years of age, this world is in for a winner. Too often we fail in our efforts because we have been brought up believing that we cannot do some things. The people who change the world are people who have taken *impossible* out of their dictionaries. The men and women who make changes in history are those who come against the odds and tell the odds that it's impossible for the odds to stop them.

To change the world, take "impossible" out of your dictionary.

DETERMINED
BY DEMANDS

*Noah did everything just as God **commanded** him*
(Genesis 6:22; 7:5,16; 21:4).

Genesis chapter 1 also teaches us that potential is determined by the demands made on it by the creator of it. This is the most amazing thing I have ever discovered about potential. The potential of a thing is determined by the demands made on it by the one who made it. A creator will not call forth from his creation something he did not put into it.

If, for example, the Ford Motor Company wanted to build a car with an engine that was supposed to have a certain degree of horsepower to get up to 200 miles per hour, they would create a car with enough spark plugs and pistons and other things to run at that speed. First they would design it. Then they would build it. Finally they would hire a professional to take it on test track to clock its speed. Because they designed and built the car to run at 200 miles per hour, they would tell the driver: "Run this car until it hits 200 miles per hour."

Now how can they demand from that car 200 miles per hour? Simple. They built into the car the ability to produce 200 miles per hour. If all other cars can only go 198 miles per hour, they have reason to believe their car will go into a race and win. They are calling forth from the car, or demanding of it, what they created it to produce.

The same is true of our relationship with God. Whenever God demands something of you, don't ask whether you can do it. When you pick up the Bible and read that you can do anything if you believe, don't argue that you can't. God believes (in fact He knows) that whatever you believe hard enough, strong enough, and committed enough can come out of you because He put it in you. Your potential, like that of any other creation, is determined by the demands of your Creator.

When God demands something of you, believe you can do it—and do it.

GOD'S MONEY-BACK GUARANTEE

Immediately the boy's father exclaimed,
"I do believe, but help me overcome my unbelief!"
(Mark 9:24)

God graciously offers you a "Money-Back Guarantee." When you buy an appliance, a manual usually comes with it that says: "Read this before you hook it up." It also says: "You've just purchased a television that can do XYZ." You've never seen the television do that before, but the manual says it can and will because the manufacturer made it possible for it to do it. At the end of the manual, there is usually a little phrase that says: "If there is any defect, return the merchandise to the manufacturer for a free replacement." The manufacturer is guaranteeing the potential of the thing.

God mercifully says to you, "If there are any defects, return to the Manufacturer." Isn't that a blessing? If you aren't working out, take your stuff back to the Chief. The Chief will work it out. "Come unto Me," God says. "I'm the only One who can fix you." God already has guaranteed what you can do.

God is good. He has built into you the potential to produce everything He calls for. When God says, "Love your enemies," don't start listing reasons why you can't. The ability to love is built in, it's there, no excuses. God wouldn't ask for it if it wasn't available. He wired you to produce everything He demands.

God also wired everything else to produce what He demands from it. God looks at a piece of fruit and says, "In you there is a tree. There is a seed in you, and that seed is a tree. It's there, and I demand what I put in." So God says, "Plant that seed and a tree has to come out; I put a tree in that seed. Before you were given the fruit, I made the seed with the tree." That's the way God thinks. Hallelujah!

God wired you to produce everything He demands.

36

WHATEVER YOU THINK

...all nations of the earth shall be blessed, because you have obeyed My voice (Genesis 22:18 NKJV).

Whether you use the ability God has deposited within you is totally up to you. How well you assume the responsibilities God gives you is not so much a question of how much you do, but rather how much of the available power you use. What you are doing is not near what your ability is. What you have accomplished is a joke when compared with what you could accomplish—you are not working enough with the power of God (emphasis on *work*).

You have a deposit of God's ability! Everyone who sets a limit on what they can do, also sets a limit on what they will do. No one can determine how much you can produce—except you and God.

So there is nothing in this world that should stop you from accomplishing and realizing and fulfilling and maximizing your full potential.

Proverbs 23:7 tells us if you can conceive it, you can do it. Obviously God is trying to communicate that you can *do* anything you can *think*. If you can conceive it, the fact that you can conceive it means you can do it. It doesn't matter if it's never been done—if you think it, you can do it. Likewise, if you never think it, you can't do it. God allows you to think only what you can do. If He doesn't allow you to think it, He knows you can't do it.

Think about the things you've been thinking recently. The fact that you thought them means you can do them. Now don't get me wrong. Thinking doesn't get it done. Thinking implies you can do it. See yourself doing the thing in your thoughts. Make your thought into an idea, and your idea into an imagination. Take that imagination and document it into a plan. Then go to it (of course with the proper rest periods). Put your plan into action. If you thought it, you can do it.

If you think it, you can do it!

FRUIT FACTS

But the fruit of the Spirit is love, joy, peace, patience, kindness, goodness, faithfulness, gentleness and self-control. Against such things there is no law (Galatians 5:22-23).

Each fruit of the Spirit is an attribute of God. God unconditionally says, "They are you." God knows you have love. He knows you have joy no matter what you are going through. God knows you have joy inside you because Christ is joy. The Bible says you *have* peace. When you are unhappy and everything is going wrong, God says, "Have peace." Peace is not a gift; it's a fruit. If God has it, you have it. We came out of God. Thus, everything that is in God is in us: love, joy, peace, patience, kindness, goodness, faithfulness, gentleness, self-control.

As Romans 5:5 puts it: "*…God has poured out His love into our hearts by the Holy Spirit…*" (NKJV). After you return to God, the Holy Spirit brings love back to your heart. It's not that you *can't* love; you just don't *want* to love. Love isn't a decision you make, because you already have it. That's why you can love your enemies.

"Oh, Lord, I can't control myself." It's not that you can't, you won't. You have self-control—it's a fruit of the Spirit. The last part of Galatians 5:23 says, *"Against such things there is no law* [or limit]." There is not one of these things you can get too much of. These things are already in you, and God is saying, "Go for it!" You don't have to pray for these things. They are already in you if Christ is in you. Your potential is everything that is in Christ.

When you face difficulties, your answer is not in your pastor. Nor is it in your counselor or the books you read. These can be helpful for input, but the answer is in you. Christ in you—not in me. I have my own Christ image. You have yours. Christ in you the hope of glory.

Your spirit connected to God's Spirit, which means you can do all things— even love your enemies.

BE STRONG AND COURAGEOUS!

*Then Moses called for Joshua, and as all Israel watched, he said to him, **"Be strong and courageous!** For you will lead these people into the land that the Lord swore to their ancestors he would give them"* (Deuteronomy 31:7 NLT).

God walked up to a young man and gave him an assignment. The young man became scared because the assignment was very big. He didn't know if he could handle it. Joshua was so afraid he actually started to become visibly frightened at the prospect of the job. Do you know what God said to that young man? "Be courageous. I command you to be courageous." What challenge do you face? What are you afraid of? Just remember, fear is necessary for courage to exist. Courage can only

DISCOVER THE HIDDEN YOU

be manifested in the presence of fear. So use fear to exercise your courage.

At first glance, that doesn't make any sense; because if Joshua was scared, he didn't have any courage. But God disagreed. The young man was commanded to display something he didn't know he had. When Joshua protested because Moses was going to turn the whole thing over to him, God said to Joshua, *"Be strong and courageous!"* (Deuteronomy 31:7). He didn't say, "I'm going to give you strength." Nor did He say, "I'm going to give you courage." God just said, "Be still. Stop trembling. Stop talking negatively. Stop being afraid. Just be strong and courageous." God knew there was strength in Joshua. He knew the potential for courage was there. God simply called it out, deep calling unto deep: "Be strong. Be courageous."

One morning I said to my little boy as he ran into the room and jumped on me, "You know, I'm holding in my hands all you haven't been yet." Although he didn't understand much of what I was saying, I was thinking about the vast amount of potential that lay within him just waiting to be used. Potential is like that. It's all you can be and become that you haven't yet experienced. Think about it. Potential is all you are capable of being or doing or reaching. You haven't done it yet, but you can do it.

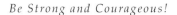

Potential is all you are capable of being or doing or reaching.

YOU CAN OVERCOME

Guide my steps by your word, so I will not be overcome by evil (Psalm 119:133 NLT).

You can overcome every habit because God has clearly stated that you can. Isn't that amazing? That's a blessing! You are not involved in a hopeless fight. Oh, please hear me if you are suffering from a bad habit. The fact that God says, "You can overcome it!" is a joy. You can beat it.

You may have resolved that you are hooked for life. That's a lie. God gave you authority over that habit when He demanded that you rule the earth (Genesis 1:26). Don't walk around with hopeless ideas: "I'll always be an addict. I'll always be an alcoholic. I'll always be like this." God has placed within you the ability to dominate everything. It is there. It is in you. The problem isn't that you *can't* control your habit; the problem is that you *won't*.

People say, "I know I shouldn't be doing this." In reality that means, "I don't want to do this. Something is wrong with this but I can't help myself." I have news for you—good news. It's more, "I haven't decided to stop doing this" than, "I shouldn't be doing this." You have what God demands. God will never demand anything He's not already provided for. Whatever God calls forth, He sees. God commanded you to dominate the earth, and the truth is you *can*.

God will never demand anything He's not already provided for. Whatever God calls forth, He sees. Stop being ruled by cocaine or marijuana. Don't be the victim of alcohol and money. They are all but leaves from the trees that we are supposed to be dominating. Don't allow yourself to be at the beck and call of a little bottle that says: "Come here—come drink me." Don't allow yourself to be controlled by marijuana leaves. The only way to escape these and other dominating unhealthy habits is to understand your purpose for being. God did not create you to be dominated by sex or chemicals. He did not create you to be *controlled* by anything. He created you so *you could control* the earth.

**Don't be a victim—
be a victor!**

THE CREAM
OF THE CROP

*Do not conform to the pattern of this world, but be
transformed by the renewing of your mind. Then
you will be able to test and approve what God's
will is—his good, pleasing and perfect will*
(Romans 12:2).

You are so much more than others expect from
you. You are so much more than you expect
from yourself. God calls us sanctified—that means
special. God calls us elite—that means cream of the
crop.

And what God calls you He sees in you. God's not
trying to conjure up things when He affirms who you
are. He already sees them in you. God looks under
all the junk and says what He sees. He says: "You
are pure. You are the righteousness of God in Christ

Jesus." He looks beneath our unrighteous behavior and sees righteousness. He sees it and calls it out. He'll keep calling it out until it reaches the surface. God's not trying to make you into something. He's trying to expose the real you He already sees. While you are walking around trying to be good and righteous, God says, "You already are righteous."

When you wake up tomorrow morning, stretch, look in the mirror and say: "You successful thing you." That's what God sees. No matter what kind of bum day is planned for you, you can decide in the morning that it's going to be a successful one. Why? Because this is the day the Lord has made. If you believe, it is possible the day will be good. It is possible to rejoice every day if you believe God has made it.

Go ahead. Stretch. Look at the success that is just waiting to happen.

God's not trying to make you into something, He wants to expose the real you He already sees.

KNOWING GOD'S THOUGHTS

[God says] *"My thoughts are not your thoughts, neither are your ways My ways"* (Isaiah 55:8).

When God told His people, that His thoughts are not our thoughts, He was not saying He doesn't want our ways and thoughts to be like His. God was telling us, "Your thoughts and ways are not like Mine, but I'm trying to get them like Mine." God wants us to have a mind like His. He told us through the apostle Paul to be transformed by the renewing of our minds. He wants you to know and obey His will—doing what is pleasing and acceptable in His sight (Romans 12:2).

What a blessing it is to know that you can wake up tomorrow morning and have God's thoughts. But too often you wake up and say: "Oh, God. It's

Monday." God says: "You're not thinking like Me. This is a day I made just for you. Come on, let's go out there and give 'em Heaven." Give 'em Heaven? Yeah, that's right. There's a world out there that is hurting. Let's go give them Heaven.

But we have the attitude: "Oh God, I can never be like You." God comes to us and says, "My child, that's exactly what I want you to do. Have the mind of Christ. Think like Me." God wants you to adopt His mind and attitude toward yourself. He desires that you think about yourself the way He does. Believe His assessment of your potential.

We have allowed the world around us to determine our potential. There are thousands of examples in history of people who were put off and cast out as misfits. Later they turned out to be some of the world's greatest leaders. We must be careful when we start putting Intelligence Quotients on people. Your potential has nothing to do with IQ tests. Only God determines your potential. Your IQ is spelled *H-O-L-Y S-P-I-R-I-T*. Your IQ is something that goes far beyond the pages of a test. It goes all the way to God.

"Come on, let's go out there and give 'em Heaven!"

SPIRITS CAN'T DIE

Now may the God of peace Himself sanctify you completely; and may your whole spirit, soul, and body be preserved blameless at the coming of our Lord Jesus Christ (1 Thessalonians 5:23 NKJV).

One day as I was talking with the Holy Spirit, He said to me, "Myles, what are you?"

I said, "Spirit."

He said, "Yea! You got that down! Do you know that spirits cannot die?"

I said, "This is true."

Then He said, "Why do humans think in terms of time only? I came back to earth to introduce humans to eternity."

I said, "Whoa!"

Then the Holy Spirit showed me how God had designed us to live forever. He said, "If you have to live forever, which you will, what are you going to do? God intended you to live forever because spirits never die. And you have to live forever being fulfilled. God never makes anything without a purpose. So you are designed to live forever and you've got to be fulfilling your purpose in life. God had to make sure He stored enough in you to last forever so you will never get bored." That blew my mind.

We are going to live forever. After a million years of worshipping and bowing and keeping company with the angels, what are we going to do? God says, "Your life is a spot in eternity—just a drop in eternity. You will not begin really living until you leave time and enter eternity."

God has packed so much into you that the book He wrote on you is only the book for time. Your potential from birth to death is contained in that book—a book so full of expectations that David says it is vast.

You don't really live until you enter eternity.

THE BOOK OF ETERNAL LIFE

All who are victorious will be clothed in white. I will never erase their names from the Book of Life, but I will announce before my Father and his angels that they are mine (Revelation 3:5 NLT).

I recently attended a function to honor a gentleman in our community—a tremendous man. Several people gave speeches about him, talking about his many accomplishments. As I sat there I thought, "Wow! If you only knew."

A booklet on the table listed all the things he had accomplished. As I looked at it I thought, "Is that all—half a page? There's a book on that man and he only has a page."

From eternity, God has been our dwelling place. Before there was anything, we were in God.

Before the mountains were born or the world was created, God existed. God was pregnant with everything, including us. We always have been. In the former state we were unseen, but we still existed. We are not haphazard. We didn't come here by mistake. From before the beginning, we were in God.

God is called the Creator because He always has something to do. God is always busy doing something. When God took us out of Himself, He gave us part of His Spirit. God is Spirit and spirits are eternal. They cannot die. Therefore, what is spirit and comes out of God is also eternal.

I believe one of God's greatest success projects is me and you. When God created human beings, He said, "This one will keep Us excited forever. Let's make and create a being in Our own image. Let's make one who will not fade away."

Mountains will fade away and rivers will run dry. Streams will evaporate and the oceans will go away. But when God came up with humans, He created something that would last forever. He took humanity out of Himself. God made you spirit and put so much into you that it will take an eternal life to live it all. *Your true potential requires eternal life to be realized and maximized.*

**You were created
for eternal life.**

NO
RETIREMENT PLAN

*Surely your goodness and unfailing love will pursue me all the days of my life, and I will **live** in the house of the Lord **forever** (Psalm 23:6 NLT).*

There are times when we get tired of our jobs. In fact, we get so tired that we look for retirement. And when we get it, we just want to retire—we want to stop permanently. God says to us, "You have it all wrong. Your thinking is wrong. There is no retirement in the Bible. It is not in My thinking." God doesn't think retirement. The only thing God thinks is rest. Why? Because God knows you have eternity to go just like He does. God wants you to assist Him in creating and developing and dominating and ruling forever and ever and ever. That's a long time. *The wealth of your potential is so rich it requires an eternal life to bring it out.*

We are not going to be in Heaven for a million years bowing down around a throne. God doesn't have an ego problem. He doesn't need us to tell Him how nice He is. In fact, He was nice without us. We make Him look pretty bad. We've really messed up God. We came out of God. We are the only ones made in His image, and look what we did. God was better off without us. He doesn't need our praises to make Him feel high.

Now don't get me wrong. I'm not talking down Heaven. I'm trying to open your mind. God has so much in store for you that He said, *"No eye has seen, no ear has heard, no mind has conceived what God has prepared for those who love Him"* (1 Corinthians 2:9). The Holy Spirit will continue to unfold it and reveal it until eternity ends—which it won't. God has placed enough potential in you to last forever. Try to do as much now as you can. Pack as much as you can into the 70 to 100 years you have here. Go for it. Go for the whole thing.

**Only God is your ability's limit.
He won't allow you to think it
if you can't do it.**

45

HOW HIGH CAN YOU JUMP?

The Lord said to me, "See, I have begun to deliver Sihon and his country over to you. Now begin to conquer and possess his land"
(Deuteronomy 2:31).

A lady lived behind our house and we would occasionally help ourselves to the fruit on her trees. One day while I was on her side of the fence, her very vicious dog suddenly appeared. I had just touched down after climbing a fruit tree. I knew I had to make a run for it. I ran toward the fence with the dog close behind me.

As the fence came closer and closer, all I could say was, "O God, I'm dead." All I could think was "jump." As I left the ground, my heart was pounding and my chest felt like an arcade full of shouting people. I was so afraid! When I landed, I was safely on the other side of the fence.

When I turned around and looked at the dog, he was barking angrily because he couldn't get over the fence. I just thought, "Yea, good for you." Suddenly I became very proud because I had gotten away from him. But when I started to realize what I had done, I looked at the fence and thought, "How did I do that?"

I thank God for that dog. He was a blessing in my life. I never jumped that high before, and I never have since, but at least I know that I did it. I discovered that day there is a lot more potential in me than I realized was there.

The same is true for you. Don't wait for a dog to teach you how to jump. Jump by your own challenge. Make a demand on yourself. Say to yourself, "I'm going to become the best in this area no matter what people have done before me." Then go after that. You will accomplish what you set out to do.

Perhaps you aren't doing more because you haven't been challenged.

46

STANDING ON THE WAVES

And when the disciples saw Him walking on the sea, they were troubled, saying, "It is a ghost!" And they cried out for fear. But immediately Jesus spoke to them, saying, "Be of good cheer! It is I; do not be afraid." And Peter answered Him and said, "Lord, if it is You, command me to come to You on the water." So He said, "Come." And when Peter had come down out of the boat, he walked on the water to go to Jesus (Matthew 14:26-29 NKJV).

One night as the disciples were crossing Lake Galilee, it was hard rowing. They were being tossed about by the waves because the wind was against them. As they struggled, a Man came toward them, walking on the water. In fear they cried out, "It's a ghost." Only when He spoke to them did the disciples recognize that it was Jesus. Peter then said, "Lord, if it's You…tell me to come to You." Jesus said "*Come!*" And Peter had the guts to respond to Jesus' order.

I believe every one of those disciples could have walked on water. The potential was in them even as it was in Peter. But only Peter succeeded, because only Peter had the guts to say, "If You challenge me, I'll take Your challenge." Although we may laugh or criticize Peter for sinking, none of us has ever walked on water. He's the only one who can say in Heaven when we get there, "I walked on water. What did you do?"

Everybody sees Jesus, but very few of us ask Jesus, "Tell me something to do. Give me something to challenge my potential." Believers are assets to the world and bring change for the better—they give their potential something to maximize. *Give your ability a responsibility*—that will change the world. There is a wealth of ability in you, but you may not have given it any responsibility. Don't die without maximizing your ability—that's irresponsible. You have no right to die with what God put in you to live out.

Don't wait to be challenged.

47

THE WORLD NEEDS YOU

So he answered and said to me: "This is the word of the Lord to Zerubbabel: 'Not by might nor by power, but by My Spirit,' says the Lord of hosts" (Zechariah 4:6 NKJV).

God has given you a skill or ability the world needs. He has been waiting for your birth. Perhaps He planted within you a unique ability to work for life. Imagine a dead baby turning purple in your hand. Others are thinking "undertaker," but you know that God has given you a potential to restore life. You believe God and pray, by the power of His Spirit, "God, this dear baby must live." Even though someone might overhear you, and that makes your prayer all the more difficult, you tap into the potential God planted deep within you and believe for the baby's life.

Miracles happen when we give our potential responsibility. God designed it that way. Don't allow the things within you to die with you because you did not challenge them. God planted the seed of potential within you. He made you according to the *potential principle*—like the rest of His creation. Don't waste that gift. Give your potential some responsibility.

People who make changes in history are those who have come against the odds and told the odds won't stop them. I read about a young boy, great mathematician, suffering from a disease that destroys his bones. He's just sort of fading away. You should see him. He looks ugly compared to what we call beauty. His glasses are falling off on the side because his face is falling in. His nose is almost gone. His teeth are all messed up. His whole body is warped. He can't write. But they say he has the greatest mathematical calculations of our day. Professors come to his home, sit at his desk, and write everything he says. They are developing mathematical books for the universities from this brain in the chair. His illness has not destroyed his potential. His genius is not affected by his physical appearance. He's a young man who is beating the odds by using all the formulas God stored within him.

**God has given you a skill or
ability the world needs.**

48

DON'T QUIT

And the Lord said to Joshua: "…You shall march around the city, all you men of war; you shall go all around the city once. This you shall do six days. …But the seventh day you shall march around the city seven times, and the priests shall blow the trumpets. …when you hear the sound of the trumpet, that all the people shall shout with a great shout; then the wall of the city will fall down flat"
(Joshua 6:1-5 NKJV).

Suppose you end up in a wheelchair next year with all the brains you have right now. Will you quit? Is your dream related to your body? Don't say "no" too fast. Some of you would just quit and get totally depressed and so sad. You'd say, "Oh, life didn't work out for me," and you'd allow all the dreams you have right now to die in the chair. You'd simply quit.

I think about President Roosevelt in a wheelchair. Did you ever think an invalid could be the president of one of the greatest nations on earth? Don't give up because you are physically handicapped. Don't give up if you are facing great odds. Your potential is not determined by whether you can see the fine print of a book, walk across the street, or lift heavy objects with both hands. Your potential is not destroyed because your mother is an alcoholic, your father's a junkie or you have no parents at all. There are many people in wheelchairs who have given up. There are many people who come from a bad family situation who have given up. Don't be one of them. Beat the odds.

Also, you will never know what you can do by using a shortcut. Shortcuts negate potential. They destroy the possibilities God planted within you. There are no shortcuts to developing your potential. Commit yourself to the long haul, the long march. Like Joshua and his army, you will be glad you did.

Never give up and never take a shortcut.

49

I'M GOING TO...

*The temple **I am going to build** will be great,*
because our God is greater than all other gods
(2 Chronicles 2:5).

My Father's house has many rooms; if that were not
*so, would I have told you that **I am going there** to*
prepare a place for you? (John 14:2).

So you are ignorant of the very thing you worship—
*and this is what **I am going to proclaim** to*
proclaim to you (Acts 17:23).

After God created Adam, He gave him a job. God knew Adam's potential to name all the animals would never be released unless it was challenged. Potential must be exercised to be fulfilled. Demands must be made on potential if it is to be released and fulfilled. God has given you potential. Unless you make demands on it, you will die with it.

Unless you venture to try things you've never done before, you'll never experience the wealth that lives within you. Decide today, "I'm going to do something I've never done before." "I'm going to get a promotion this year in my job." "I'm going to win more people to Jesus this year than my church and my pastor ever did." If you have a business, resolve to cut the overhead and increase service. Give your potential some demands. It needs to be maximized and challenged.

The greatest works in the world will be done by people who don't care who gets the credit. I don't want to be famous; *I just want to be faithful.* I don't want to be well-known; *I want to be well-used.* I don't want to be powerful; *I want to be potent.* Success requires striking out on new paths instead of traveling those that are well-worn.

Genius is 1 percent inspiration and 99 percent perspiration. There are many people with great ideas, but they have no desire to try. There are four steps to the accomplishment of your dream: 1) prepare prayerfully; 2) plan purposefully; 3) proceed positively; 4) pursue persistently.

Failure is the path of least persistence.

50

DON'T BE AFRAID TO TRY

*Even as **I try** to please everyone in every way. For I am not seeking my own good but the good of many, so that they may be saved* (1 Corinthians 10:33).

No one can climb beyond the limitations they have placed on themselves. Success is never final—failure is never fatal. Courage counts—and the willingness to move on. A great deal of talent is lost to the world for want of a little courage. Every day sends to the grave, obscure people who allowed fear and timidity to prevent them from making their first attempt to do something. Never tell a person that something can't be done, because God may have been waiting for centuries for someone to believe that the impossible is possible.

The poorest of people are those without a dream. Don't be so afraid of failure that you refuse to try. Demand something of yourself. Failure is only an incident. There's more than the failure—there's success deep behind every failure. Failure is the opportunity to more intelligently begin again. Don't be paralyzed by the failure.

Failure is proof that you tried. The greatest mistake you can make is to be afraid of making one. People who do nothing in life are those who do nothing. Challenge your potential. Demand things of yourself that are beyond what you have already done. Expect more from yourself than the accomplishments that are easily within your reach. What you have is not all you are. The limit of your potential is God. It is better to attempt a thing and fail, than to never try and not know you could succeed.

Principles for discovering the hidden you: Believe there is potential in you to accomplish something worthwhile. Unless you use your potential, you will never realize how much ability is inside you. Jump by your own challenge. Don't wait for someone to challenge you. Don't let the odds that are against you stop you from fulfilling your potential. Shortcuts negate your ability. Don't be so afraid of failure that you refuse to try.

**Success is never final—
failure is never fatal.**

THE VINE AND THE BRANCHES

[Jesus says] *"I am the true vine, and My Father is the vinedresser. Every branch in Me that does not bear fruit He takes away; and every branch that bears fruit He prunes, that it may bear more fruit. You are already clean because of the word which I have spoken to you. Abide in Me, and I in you. As the branch cannot bear fruit of itself, unless it abides in the vine, neither can you, unless you abide in Me"* (John 15:1-4 NKJV).

A grapevine is an interesting plant. The vine, which is the thick wooden part running from the ground up the pole, is the only part of the plant that contains life ability. None of the life is in the branches; all of it is in the vine. There is no life in the little green things you see on the side with the grapes hanging on them. They are getting their life from the vine. They have no root in themselves. If you were to break one of those green branches off and plant it in the ground, it would never grow because it has no life ability in it. Each small branch depends on the life flowing up and down the great branch, the vine, to give it life. Thus, the branches cannot live without the vine. The relationship of the vine and its branches is reflected throughout God's creation. Life is not possible when a thing is separated from its source.

If you decide you don't need God, you also have decided never to become all you are capable of being. Like the branches of the grapevine, our life depends upon our Source. When God wanted human beings, He spoke to Himself—God is our Source. We came out of God and contain a measure of His ability. But our only hope of fulfilling that ability lies in God. We must be connected to God if we are going to tap any of our true potential. Jesus came to bring us back to God so God's original intention could be fulfilled. So, the key to your full potential is staying connected to God.

Attach yourself to your Source to fulfill your potential.

THE TRUE VINE

I am the true vine, and My Father is the gardener.
He cuts off every branch in me that bears no fruit,
while every branch that does bear fruit he prunes
(John 15:1-2).

As a plant can't fulfill its potential without being in relationship with the soil, you cannot fulfill your true potential without being connected to God. Jesus calls Himself the *true vine* because there are a lot of other vines around to get hooked onto: education, philosophy, science, even religion. The word *vine* here literally means "source of life." Like the grapevine for its branches, Jesus is our Source of life. If you depend on financial wealthy or education, all you will have is what education can offer—an intellectual stimulation. Jesus says, *"I am the True Vine."* By this statement He implies that there are vines or sources that are not true or genuine.

Like a gardener in the vineyard, your heavenly Father comes into your life and starts clipping at the habits that are hanging on and the attitudes that are killing you. He trims a little bit here and a little bit there from the bad relationships stunting your potential and restricting your growth.

The Gardener says, "You can do better than you are doing." *Clip.* "Stop lying." *Clip.* "Stop disobeying me." *Clip.* Carefully and steadily, God cuts off whatever is holding you back, because He knows you are not living up to your possibilities. He knows you're not measuring up to your Source.

Do you need to quit a habit or two so your life more truly reflects the potential of the One who made you? Are you wasting time feeling guilty about sin? How many hours in a day are you losing to disobedience and rebellion? Prune your life through discipline and obedience to God, who desires your potential to be maximized. Remember, all God's commands and laws are given to maximize your performance and free your potential.

Your Father is your Gardener—submit to His pruning with joy.

FREEDOM TO OBEY

…You are free to eat from any tree in the garden; but you must not eat from the tree of the knowledge of good and evil, for when you eat from it you will certainly die (Genesis 2:16-17).

God gives you freedom, but He also puts some limitations on you. Whenever you violate your limitations, you are in rebellion against God. The only limitations of your potential are violations of God's Word. If you do anything that doesn't violate the Word of God, you are within your freedom. God gives you freedom to do anything except disobey Him. That's a tremendous freedom. You are free to do anything within the context of God's Word. If God says it's cool, go for it, because the possibilities of your life are all connected with God.

God comes into your life with pruning shearers to free you from your disobedience and rebellion.

He comes to take out those things that are stopping you from developing and growing and obeying. Imagine how different your life might have been if you had not wasted months or years on a particular habit. Imagine how different your life could be if you would let go of a grudge or clean up your language.

Anything that is contrary to the Word of God is subject to God's pruning. He comes into your life to help you clean up your act. He wants you to enjoy the freedom of obedience and life within His limitations. Bearing a pruning shear, God trims the useless and dead wood from your life so you can draw from Him the fresh fullness of your potential.

Then Jesus says, "Okay, you're clean. I've saved you. You're hooked up, straightened out, and fixed. You know who your Source is. Now stay that way by remaining attached to Me." You are cleansed through the word Jesus speaks to you when you ask Him to forgive you. You are clean and free to do *anything* that doesn't violate God's Word—free to be all you were created to be and do (whatever He says you can do). What freedom!—freedom that lasts as long as you remain connected to God.

God gives you freedom to do anything except disobey Him.

54

WHATEVER YOU WISH

Jesus says, "If you remain in me and my words remain in you, ask whatever you wish, and it will be done for you" (John 15:7).

No matter how talented or gifted you are, you will never be truly fulfilled and successful apart from a personal relationship with your Creator-Source. Jesus' words in John 15:7 are almost frightening—*whatever you wish*. God will give you whatever you ask for so long as you remain in Him. What a promise! When you open your life completely to God, the Holy Spirit's crowbar firmly resists satan's attempt to recap your well. The wealth of your potential becomes limitless and free. Whatever you imagine will be done, because God won't allow you to think it unless you can do it.

So, the secret to a happy, productive life is remaining attached to your Divine Source. If you abide in Christ, His word will abide in you. You can ask whatever you wish and it will be given to you. God will provide from the depths of His grace—freely, abundantly, victoriously. You don't have to hustle. You don't have to plead. God is always waiting to help you live a full, fruitful, complete life. From His storehouse of riches, God will supply all you can imagine, and more because *He wants you to fulfill your potential*. As you remain attached to the Vine and submitted to the discipline of the Gardener, you will know God's blessings.

God created you to exalt and bring glory to His name. When you bear fruit, God is glorified. His name is exalted whenever you use the abilities He stored in you. The whole purpose for your being— to reflect and increase the glory of God—is fulfilled whenever you maximize your potential.

Principles for discovering the hidden you: What God speaks to is the source for what He creates.

Jesus is your Source of life. God prunes your life to bring you into the freedom of obedience. The key to fulfilling your potential is staying attached to God. Only disciples committed to abiding in Christ will maximize their potential. God is glorified when you use your abilities.

God is depending on you to fill the earth with His glory.

55

POTENTIAL
POTENCY

*And the child grew, and she brought him to
Pharaoh's daughter, and he became her son.... Now
it came to pass in those days, when Moses was
grown.... And Moses said to the people: "Remember
this day in which you went out of Egypt, out of the
house of bondage; for by strength of hand the
Lord brought you out of this place"*
(Exodus 2:10-11; Exodus 13:3 NKJV).

Discussing our true and full potential, it is essential that we come to appreciate how important each one of us is and how special we are to God. If you were aware of how much power and worth you have, the first thing that would be affected would be your attitude toward yourself.

Many of us have a difficult time projecting a good attitude toward others because we feel bad about ourselves. Great positive thinkers and personal motivators, along with psychologists, all agree that if you feel good about yourself, then your attitude toward others will be influenced by that attitude. However, for many positive thinking programs, this is simply an attempt to convince ourselves by mental assent that we are of value and worth. It's an attempt to convince you of something you don't believe.

On the contrary, we are talking here about a fact grounded in truth and reality, and established by the One who created you. Your worth, value, and potential have all been given by God, and there is no formula, test, or scheme to measure the full extent of these qualities and abilities.

Your true ability and potential should not be measured by the limitations of an academic test or an Intelligence Quotient score. Nor should it be determined by the social, cultural, economic, and educational "norms" of your society. Society did not create you. You are not a product of your culture. You are not the offspring of your economy. You were not created by the Department of Education. Therefore, none of these has the right to determine how much potential you really possess. If you want to know how much potential you have, first discover who created or manufactured you. Then check the demands He is making upon your life. Whatever He is demanding of you, *you can do.*

To discover how much potential you have, discover your Creator.

56

YOUR TRIUNE SELF

*Now may the God of peace Himself sanctify you completely; and may your whole **spirit**, **soul**, and **body** be preserved blameless at the coming of our Lord Jesus Christ* (1 Thessalonians 5:23 NKJV).

Humans are triune beings created after the image and likeness of our Creator-Source. We consist of three distinct yet intricately related dimensions—spirit, soul, and body. Each dimension is designed to fulfill a specific purpose in God's plan for His creation. Each realm of humankind is designed with the potential to maximize its function and fulfill its intended purpose. But the potential of each dimension cannot be understood apart from its Source.

Despite our technological advancements and scientific explorations of this masterpiece of creation, scientists continue to admit that they have limited knowledge concerning the potential of this mechanism of precision we call *the human body*.

When God created Adam, He created him a *spirit* being with a *physical* house (body). Then God placed him on the *physical* earth. God purposed and intended to rule and dominate the physical realm from the invisible realm through the agency of *humankind*. In essence, God desired to control the *seen* from the *unseen* through the *unseen* living in the *seen* on the *seen*. God desired to have His Kingdom extended from Heaven to earth by allowing His Spirit to reign through a human's spirit as humankind dominated the earth through souls and manifested His nature through our bodies.

Therefore, the triune nature of humans is designed for the following purposes: 1) *spirit*, to relate to God (pick up the spirit world); 2) *soul*, to relate to the mental realm (intelligence); 3) *body*, to relate to the physical environment (pick up earth).

The human body was specifically designed to relate to and pick up the earth or physical realm. God did not intend the body to relate to the spiritual or supernatural world. For this reason, our five senses—powers of sight, touch, hearing, smell, and taste—are all related to the natural, physical world.

The potential of our bodies is governed by its physical capabilities. God never intended for us to be controlled or limited by our physical body.

You were not created to be intimidated by your environment.

OUR MEASURE OF REALITY

Then the eyes of both of them were opened, and
they realized they were naked (Genesis 3:7).

The human original state in the garden of Eden, before the fall, was one of perfect union and fellowship with God. Adam was designed to live from the *inside* to the *outside*, from his *spirit* to his *body*. God designed humans to be *led* by their spirit, not *driven* by the environment. We were intended to live through spiritual *discernment*, not physical *senses*. But when Adam (the first man) disobeyed God, he destroyed his fellowship and communion with the Spirit of God (Genesis 3). The consequence was death.

Death is isolation from the spirit world of God. Through disobedience, our spirit lost contact with the Source of Heaven. As a result, we became victims of our *soul* (mind, will, emotions) and *body* (five senses). Our lives are governed by our external environment as our five senses control our existence.

Immediately after Adam and Eve disobeyed God's command, their eyes were opened (Genesis 3:7). In essence, Adam and Eve suddenly became aware of their external environment. They began to live life from the knowledge they gained from their *senses*. That was the birth of education.

From that day on, humans measure their lives, worth, and value by their environment. And the relationship between humans and our environment gave birth to humanistic philosophy. In reality, the body and its sensual capacity became our measure of reality. We started living and interpreting our existence according to the *information* we gain through the senses of our *body*, instead of the *revelation* received through our spirit, from the Spirit of God. This change has caused humankind to limit our potential ability to the capabilities of our senses and physical body.

Don't become a victim of your soul (mind, will, emotions) or body (five senses).

58

YOUR BODY IS NOT YOUR TRUE SELF

And Mephibosheth, who was crippled in both feet,
lived in Jerusalem and ate regularly at the
king's table (2 Samuel 9:13 NLT).

There are millions of physically handicapped individuals who, because of their society's concept of potential, have resigned themselves to a life of self-pity, depression, and isolation. There are many who have confused their bodies with their true selves. They have mistaken the "house" for the "resident."

But history gives ample evidence of thousands who have freed themselves of the myth that their bodies should dictate their true potential. They have defied the limitations of their "dirt houses" and soared to the unlimited heights of their soul's and spirit's potential. Many have turned their wheelchairs into the cockpits of jetliners as they explored the heights of their capabilities. Other have used their walking canes to pole vault them into positions that changed the world. Some transformed their world of silence to produce sounds that many are enjoying today. Still others have used their blindness to see beyond the physical. They have captured sights others long to see.

Helen Keller refused to be blinded by others' opinions of her ability—she changed the attitude of the world. Sir Winston Churchill refused to be muted by his speech impediment and physical handicap. While a member of the British Parliament and later the Prime Minister of Britain, he delivered some of history's most life-changing speeches.

What is your handicap? Is it a wheelchair, a bed, a walker, the socioeconomic status of your family, or the color of your skin? Is it the ghetto, your parents' lifestyle, the level of your education, or a terminal illness? Are you disabled by divorce, the absence of your parents, incest, or child abuse? Are you blind or deaf? Do you have a speech impediment or a poor self-esteem? Whatever your *perceived* handicap may be, you must never allow your true potential to become a victim of the limitations of your physical body or your environment.

**Reach beyond your grasp.
Your body is not your full potential.**

59

YOUR BODY—GOD'S TEMPLE

*Therefore we do not lose heart. Though outwardly
we are wasting away, yet inwardly we are being
renewed day by day* (2 Corinthians 4:16).

I encourage you to develop and maintain a correct attitude toward your body. Learn to see it from the perspective of God, its Creator, who (through the apostle Paul) calls it *"the temple of the living God"* (2 Corinthians 6:16). God admonishes you to keep your temple holy, clean, and healthy. Its maintenance and effective operation are your responsibility. Like any essential equipment, your body needs regular checkups, proper amounts of food, periods of recuperation and recreation, and invigorating exercise. But do not allow your body to become the dictator of your potential. You are not your body.

The biblical perspective on the body is revealed in a number of clear declarations including: *"Do you not know that your body is a temple of the Holy Spirit, who is in you…? …Therefore honor God with your body"* (1 Corinthians 6:19-20).

If we determine our potential by the condition of our bodies—whether we are handicapped or relatively healthy and fit—we are still relying on a premise that is constantly dissolving. You and I must not allow any physical impediment or the natural aging process to immobilize the potential that lies within us.

The apostle Paul writes of Abraham:

As it is written: "I have made you a father of many nations." He is our father in the sight of God, in whom he believed…. Against all hope, Abraham in hope believed and so became the father of many nations…. Without weakening in his faith, he faced the fact that his body was as good as dead…being fully persuaded that God had the power to do what he had promised (Romans 4:17-21).

The key to Abraham's success is related to his attitude toward his body. The demands made upon him by God were beyond the natural capacity of his physical body. He was handicapped by age and his wife had a barren womb. But they believed that God had provided the potential to fulfill the demand.

Refuse to limit your true potential by the limitations of your physical body.

60

THE SOUL'S POTENTIAL

*And what do you benefit if you gain the whole world
but lose your own **soul**? Is anything worth more
than your **soul**? (Matthew 16:26 NLT).*

Some years ago a famous pop singer sang a song titled "I'm a Soul Man." That title became a common phrase throughout the Western world. I suspect he was referring to the cultural-ethnic orientation of the African American artistic expression. But the statement communicates both a statement of truth and a myth. As discussed earlier, the *soul* is the triunity of the *mind*, the *will* and the *emotions*. The soul was created for the purpose of receiving *revelation* from the spirit to communicate it to the body and *information* from the physical senses to transmit it to the spirit.

In essence, the soul was designed to be the "servant" of our spirit, and the body was designed to be the "servant" of the soul. A human is a spirit, lives in a body, and possesses a soul. But the fall of humankind changed that.

When Adam disobeyed God's words, his spirit lost fellowship with God's Spirit and was paralyzed. The soul became a victim of his body and the physical senses. When *revelation* from our spirit was replaced by *information* from the physical senses, we became victims of our environment with education as the primary goal. In fact, we were reduced to a "soul man."

Never allow a teacher's opinion or the score on an academic test or the fact that you didn't complete your formal education to dictate the magnitude of your potential. You are as potent as your Creator says you are. The exercise of the soul can make you smart, but not wise. Paul states in First Corinthians 1:25: *"For the foolishness of God is wiser than human wisdom, and the weakness of God is stronger than human strength."*

A human is a spirit that lives in a body and possesses a soul.

YOUR SPIRIT'S POTENTIAL

*Those who live according to the sinful nature have
their minds set on what that nature desires; but
those who live in accordance with the **Spirit** have
their minds set on what the **Spirit** desires*
(Romans 8:5).

The measure of your true potential is your spirit.
God has always intended that you and I would
live from the inside—from the spirit in communion
with the eternal Spirit of God. Without that relationship, you are limited to the potential of your soul
and your body. The apostle Paul in his letter to the
church at Rome wrote: *"The **mind** governed by the
flesh is death, but the **mind** governed by the Spirit is life
and peace"* (Romans 8:6).

I believe the Spirit of God has desires, which are God's original predestined will for your life as written in Psalm 139:16. If you allow the Holy Spirit to fellowship with and minister to your spirit, and you remain connected to the Source of your potential, then you will live according to the knowledge of God's revelation of your true potential. There are things in God's mind concerning you that your soul can never receive, because it cannot discern them. God has information on your ability and potential that will astonish you and your family. Paul mentions this in First Corinthians 2:9-11:

However as it is written: "What no eye has seen, what no ear has heard, and what no human mind has conceived"—the things God has prepared for those who love him—these are the things God has revealed to us by his Spirit. The Spirit searches all things, even the deep things of God. For who knows a person's thoughts except their own spirit within them? In the same way no one knows the thoughts of God except the Spirit of God.

Principles for discovering the hidden you: The key to knowing your true potential is to know your Source—God. Humans are triune beings: body, soul and spirit. The spirit is intended to relate to God, the soul to the mental realm, and the body to the physical environment. Death is isolation from the spirit world.

The measure of your true potential is your spirit.

READ THE INSTRUCTIONS— THE BIBLE

Jesus replied, "You are in error because you do not know the Scriptures or the power of God"
(Matthew 22:29).

If you want a piece of equipment to operate at its maximum potential, you have to follow the manufacturer's instructions. If you don't follow the instructions, you may damage the product—or at least you won't know what you can expect from it. Only if you follow the instructions can you expect the product to meet the demands specified by the manufacturer—demands that equal what the manufacturer designed and built into the product.

When God first presented this piece of equipment called man, something went wrong. Instead of taking it back to the manufacturer to be fixed, we took it to a second-rate, second-class, unskilled technician. And look what he did. He muddled the job. We submitted God's equipment and product to satan, who is an unauthorized dealer with no genuine parts.

But God loved us so much that, even though the warranty had run out, He decided to take back the product. Though someone else has tried to fix us and has messed us up, God is starting all over again—and He's putting in His own parts. God is rebuilding and remaking us. He knows us better than anybody else, because He is our Creator. His Word, the Bible, reveals much about His attitude toward our potential.

God created you to rule over all the earth and everything that creeps in it. He will never demand anything of you He didn't already build into you. Thus, if the earth in any way is dominating you, you are malfunctioning. You were not created to give into cigarettes or submit to alcohol. God did not intend for you to be controlled by drugs, sex, money, power, or greed. If any of these are governing you, you are living below your privilege. Because God has already declared it to be so, you have the ability to dominate the earth. Everything in the earth must be under your subjection, not mastering you.

Even Jesus
read the Scriptures!

YOUR BUILT-INS
CAME STANDARD

God blessed them and said to them, "Be fruitful and increase in number; fill the earth and subdue it"
(Genesis 1:28).

Again, God is calling forth something that's already in you. He didn't tell the man and the woman to *try* to be fruitful, He simply told them to *be fruitful*. He knew they already had the ability to multiply and reproduce and fill the earth. You too can reproduce yourself. He always places the potential inside before He calls it forth. Whatever God calls you to do, He has already built in.

God gave you the ability to imagine and plan and bring into being anything you desire. If you want to do anything, God already said, "You can do it." Only if you lack the commitment to follow after your dream will your dream remain unfinished. The potential to do and plan is in you already—if you believe and persevere.

"Everything is possible for him who believes" (Mark 9:23). Not only are you able to plan, but you also have the ability to believe something that seems impossible and actually make it possible. If you can abandon yourself to an idea and sacrifice all you have for that idea, God says, "It's possible for that idea to come to pass."

"I will give you the keys of the kingdom of heaven; whatever you bind on earth will be bound in heaven, and whatever you loose on earth will be loosed in heaven" (Matthew 16:19). Jesus is talking here about your power to influence what's on earth as well as what's in Heaven. If you bind something on earth, it will be bound in Heaven. You have influence in Heaven. Likewise, if you loose something on earth, Heaven has to do the same thing—loose it. You may never have imagined that you possess that kind of power. But Jesus says you do.

You have the power to influence both realms of earth and Heaven.

GREATER WORKS THAN JESUS

*Jesus says, "I tell you the truth, **anyone who
believes** in me will do the same works I have done,
and even greater works, because I am going to be
with the Father"* (John 14:12 NLT).

Jesus sees in you the potential to do greater things
than He did. And He means what He says. For
many years I didn't want to read that Scripture
because I knew that what Jesus said and what was
really happening were two different things. But
if Jesus says you have that potential, it's in there
somewhere. Remember, whatever God says, you
can do. He won't ask you to do anything He hasn't
already wired you to do.

God believes in you. He knows the vastness of
your potential. If He gives you an assignment, He's

already given you the ability to fulfill what He asks. Along with His demand always comes the capability to meet that demand. But remember: To release your potential, you must be related to your Source. Only as you are connected to God, can you fulfill and maximize your true potential.

Sin, or rebellion against God, clogs up our potential. Disobedience to God may have stunted your capacity for growth. But God sees and cares about that problem. He sent Jesus into the world to die for you. Jesus doesn't have a problem knowing who He is and what He can do. *You* have that problem. Jesus came to die so *you* can know who you are and what is the fullness of *your* potential. He came to open the capacity of who you are—to unclog your true self.

Calvary is God's way of providing the means to unplug your true potential. Because disobedience has capped off your potential, God offers you forgiveness and hope through Jesus Christ. When plugged up, you can't begin to touch your true ability. Only after you say "yes" to Jesus and your spirit begins to communicate and fellowship again with the Holy Spirit, can you start the journey of fulfilling all the potential God planted within you before you were born.

**Say yes to Jesus and
release your true self.**

65

YOUR GODLY PURPOSE

*At one time all the people of the world spoke the
same language and used the same words. …They
began saying to each other, "Let's make bricks and
harden them with fire." …Then they said, "Come,
let's build a great city for ourselves with a tower
that reaches into the sky. This will make us famous
and keep us from being scattered all over the world"*
(Genesis 11:1-4 NLT).

The Bible tells us a story about people who decided to build a city with a tower that reached to the heavens. They wanted to be *"famous."* When God saw how committed the builders were to their task He said, *"…nothing they plan to do will be impossible for them."* So He came down and confused their languages so they couldn't work together. That stopped their building (Genesis 11:8).

Do you think God was against the tower? No. God was *against the goal* of the tower. They did not have a relationship with God. They were ungodly people who intended to build a tower to Heaven so *their* name could be great. They weren't interested in making God's name great; they wanted to make a name for themselves, they wanted to be famous.

When God saw how committed they were to their task, He knew He had to stop them. Otherwise, they would be able to do anything they wanted to do. God made this declaration to people who had no relationship with Him. Yet He saw in them the potential to do much. He knew the potential, ability, and untapped power He had placed within all humanity.

Think then what you can do if you are attached to your Source. Jesus came into the world to reestablish your connection with God. He came to show you who you really are underneath the cap of sin and disobedience. He came to teach you how to look beyond the realm of the visible into the unseen sphere of faith.

Human potential without godly purpose produces self-destruction.

66

DO ALL
YOU CAN DREAM

*He had a **dream** in which he saw a stairway resting
on the earth, with its top reaching to heaven, and the
angels of God were ascending and descending on it*
(Genesis 28:12).

Man has accomplished many things without God. Many inventors in the world are
ungodly people. Most of the people who do great
feats and accomplish great exploits are ungodly
people. Imagine what would happen if they were
connected to God. Jesus came to provide that
hookup. When God saw what we could and should
do, it disappointed Him that we were not aware of
it. So He paid the greatest price necessary— the cost
of His own life—to release our full potential. Then
He said, "Now go on, son. Do all you can dream. If
you can think it, daughter, you can do it."

God paid the greatest price necessary—the cost of His own life—to release our full potential.

Yet many of us still live below the level of our true ability. We have settled for the standards established by the opinions of others regarding our potential. We are afraid to move beyond our dreams to action. It is more comfortable to think about all we *might* do instead of working to achieve what we *can* do. People who change the world are people who stop dreaming and wake up. They don't just wish, they act.

If you have accepted Jesus as your Lord and Savior, I'm here to encourage you to move on with the real things of God. What have you done since you were saved? What have you accomplished?

In the sixth chapter of Matthew, Jesus challenges that thought pattern. He instructs us to live from the perspective of what exists that we cannot see, instead of being totally caught up in the details and needs of our daily lives. God lives and thinks in the potential. He always sees things that have not yet been manifested. Faith too lives in the potential not in the present. Jesus simply asks us to have faith—to believe in God's goodness and care.

**Life is more than
shelter, food, and security.**

STOP
WORRYING

*Can any one of you by worrying add a single
hour to your life?* (Matthew 6:27)

Jesus was talking to His disciples, not to the multitudes. His words were for people who had already left home and family and everything to follow Him. But He says, "Here you are. You've left children. You've given up your job. You say you love Me, but yet you worry. Don't you know that God is aware of all your needs? Don't you see how He takes care of the birds of the air and the grass of the field? How much more precious you are to your heavenly Father than these. Stop worrying. Stop babbling on like the pagans. You are supposed to be living in God's Kingdom. I have come into the world to reestablish and build back God's Kingdom."

In teaching His followers that food, drink, clothes, and shelter are not the most important things in life, Jesus directly contradicts the psychological theories of our world. He dares you to follow God and think in the opposite. God doesn't start with your wants, but with who you are. God wants you to first know who you are. Then you will realize you deserve the things. In God's design, you deserve the things because you are somebody.

There are people who have everything, but they still don't know who they are. People accumulate things with the hope that the things will make them somebody. But you don't become somebody by accumulating things. Ask the guy at the top who can't sleep. Ask the guy who has everything except peace and love and joy in his heart. God desires to give you self-worth and self-esteem first. He wants you to know who you are first.

I have met so many people who have everything except the knowledge of who they are. Jesus says, "Why worry about these things? Life is so much more than these things about which you worry. Life is peace and love and joy and patience and gentleness…."

You don't need things to enjoy life—
you need life to enjoy things.

68

MIND CONTROL

*Therefore do not **worry** about tomorrow,*
*for tomorrow will **worry** about itself*
(Matthew 6:34).

Seek first the things of God and everything else you need will fall into place. The mind controlled by the Spirit of God is full of life and peace. Peace is so important to a fulfilled life. It goes hand in hand with the life Jesus came to bring. You don't have to worry when you know what is coming. When you live by the Spirit in the realm of the unseen and the invisible, there is no reason to worry. God is holding what is in store for you, because all things that are, were and are in God.

If you'll let Him, God will work it all out for you. Through your spirit talking with His Spirit, He'll assure you everything is going to be okay. You don't have to worry if God's already told you how a particular situation is going to turn out. Relax and commit yourself to maximize your potential. Preoccupy yourself with this assignment and purpose for your life, knowing that whatever God asks for He provides for.

When we are distracted by our drive for personal security and our search for identity, we rarely achieve our true potential. Our search for things, what we can relate to through our senses and our minds, harasses us and keeps us so busy trying to make a living that we don't have time to live. We are so caught up trying to make it *through* life that we don't have time to be *in* life.

God wants all He stored in you to blossom and flourish. He longs for the relationship between your spirit and His Holy Spirit to prosper so you can reveal the limitless depths of the wealth of your hidden potential. God never put anything into you that was not supposed to come out of you. His joy is fulfilled when you show off His glory—the real nature of who God is.

The summit of God's desires for your life is that you will show through your being who He is.

69

EVERYDAY FAITH

*But all of you who were **faithful** to the Lord
your God are still alive today—every one of you*
(Deuteronomy 4:4 NLT).

God is waiting for you to ask Him for everything you need. But you have to ask with faith,
because faith is the stuff that deals with unseen
things. Faith is not some spooky experience. It's
simply knowing that what you can't see is there.

Can you imagine waking up every day, with all
your problems, knowing that whatever you see is
not the real story? Can you even imagine living
that way—looking not at things that can be seen,
but at the things that are not seen? What we see
is temporary. It's those things we can't see that
are eternal. Living by faith requires looking at the
unseen, because everything that is, was in God; and

everything you could be is in you now, waiting for you to make demands on it by faith in God.

How often have you had a good idea and done nothing about it because you didn't desire it badly enough? When we want something so badly we can taste it, an urgency energizes our efforts. This is extremely important for your faith, because faith is what you are asking for but can't yet see. A strong desire enables you to stand your ground until you see what you have believed. There are only a few who are gutsy enough to live in this manner. How much do you really desire the goals you have set for your life?

God is pregnant with everything that isn't yet visible—including what you ask for in prayer. When you ask for something in faith, it is already on the way. You can't see it, but if you believe, it is already in process. God wants you to ask many things of Him, because He is full with many blessings and abilities that He wants to release.

How much do you really desire the goals you have set for your life?

A CRAVING DESIRE

*Therefore I say unto you, What things soever ye
desire, when ye pray, believe that ye receive
them, and ye shall have them*
(Mark 11:24 King James Version).

Thus, whatever you *desire* when you pray, you shall have—*but only what you desire*. Not what you *pray* for—only what you *desire when you pray*. There are many things we ask God for in prayer that we don't really desire. We don't crave them at the expense of life. We don't want them bad enough to sacrifice for them. We just hope God does it. If it happens, praise the Lord; if it doesn't happen, praise the Lord. When you pray with this attitude, you don't really want what you prayed for. If you truly want something when you pray, Jesus says you'll get up and knock and seek and run out until you get it (Matthew 7:7-8). If you are serious about *desiring* what you pray for, you will get up off your knees and go do it.

Many people get distracted in life because they do not desire anything enough to keep on course. If you do not set a goal for your potential and say, "Look, I don't care what anybody says. That's what I want to become," you might as well forget it. You must have a goal that you desire so strongly you will go after it no matter what the expense. If you are not willing to do that, you have lost already, because it is your desire for the thing that will keep you on the road of consistency. Potential needs desire to place demands on it.

This life is full of advertisements for your attention. Life is crowded and jammed with distractions. They come from all sides, trying to shake you from your goal. If you don't have a goal, they will provide one for you. You must know where you want to go and what you want to become. Potential needs purpose to give it direction.

When you pray, desire what you ask for. Refuse to be distracted or interrupted. The power of your potential will be revealed as you sacrifice everything to attain what you desired in prayer.

**Your desire controls
your direction in life.**

FOLLOW THE NARROW ROAD

*But small is the gate and narrow the road that leads
to life, and only a few find it* (Matthew 7:14).

Unfortunately, most of us will never fulfill the deepest desires of God's heart. Though He has done His best to free us from the false attitudes and perceptions that keep us from achieving our real potential, God is often disappointed by the lives of His creatures.

Perhaps you are a parent who has tried and tried and tried and still your kids haven't worked out. You've tried your best and given your best, but they still have disappointed you. Sometimes pastors also feel that way. They give and give and give, and the people still disappoint them. And often some of the ones who are messing up the most are the ones to whom they have given the most. Each of us feels the hurt when the people we love and have tried to help, struggle in the gutter, their lives in ruins.

In Matthew 7, Jesus predicts that many will hear His message, but few will follow Him and obey. Many will reject—or simply fail to accept—the abundant life He came to offer.

Enter through the narrow gate. For wide is the gate and broad is the road that leads to destruction, and many enter through it. But small is the gate and narrow the road that leads to life, and only a few find it (Matthew 7:13-14).

Those words have saved my sanity. I want all who read this devotional to fulfill their potential; but I know only a few will. Many people will never fulfill their purpose in life. If only I could take my desire and put it into every reader, I'd do it. But I can't. Some will end up in the gutter because they won't receive and practice what God is saying. Whether you fail or succeed, win or lose, does not depend on God—but on you.

**God is ready to do His part if
you are willing to cooperate with
His purpose for your life.**

BE ONE OF THE FEW

Yet to all who did receive him, to those who believed in his name, he gave the right to become children of God (John 1:12).

Not everyone will look for the things God planted within them to be used for His glory. Not everyone will choose to fulfill their potential. Indeed, the number will be few. I wonder which category you are in.

Where you are? Are you in the broad gate where everybody is going nowhere? Come, join those at the narrow gate. Be one of the few. Choose to separate yourself, square your shoulders and do something. Choose to be someone. Leave your footprints in the sands of history and carry none of your potential to the cemetery.

Are you a can-do person? Are you brave enough to face the challenge and take the risk to be effective?

Will you dare to believe the impossible no matter what others say? I hope so. The world desperately needs some people who will go for the miracles no matter what it takes. The world needs some people who will believe God for the potential buried within them—desiring their dreams enough to move out and act. Only a few will find the kind of potential that allows them to live from the depths of their hidden ability. But for those who do, deep wells of possibilities will come to light as God reveals to them more and more of what He planned before the foundations of the world.

Join the few. Release the miracles hidden in your thoughts. Dare to try even after you've failed. Become reconnected to God and find out who you are and what you can do. Give your potential a chance, because God is waiting to do much more than you can think or imagine. He loves you. He wants you to be the beautiful person He created you to be.

Join the few—the beloved of Christ.

THE WORLD VIEW

Do not pervert justice; do not show partiality to the poor or favoritism to the great, but judge your neighbor fairly (Leviticus 19:15).

Today there are almost 8 billion people on planet Earth. Over half of these people live in countries and conditions that have been labeled *Third World*. This term was invented by a French economist who was attempting to describe the various groupings of peoples throughout the world based on their socio-economic status. Whether or not this term is valid, it is generally accepted as a description or element of identification for millions of people.

I was born and live in a part of the world that is said to fall within this category. The term is defined as any people who did not benefit from or participate in the industrial revolution. A large majority of these people were not allowed to benefit from or participate in the industrial revolution because they were subjugated at that time, being used to fuel the economic base for that revolution. Many of them were reduced to slaves and indentured servants, thus robbing them of their identity, dignity, self-worth, and self-respect.

With this prejudice in mind, I wish to say to all Third World peoples everywhere—black, yellow, brown, red, and white; African, American, Indian, Spanish, Latin, Arabian, Oriental, and other nationalities—your potential is limitless. You possess the ability to achieve, develop, accomplish, produce, create, and perform anything your mind can conceive. God created you the way you are, with all the potential you need deposited within you so you can fulfill your potential in this life. The opinions of others should never determine your self-worth. Your identity is not found in the prejudgments of others, but in the Source from which you came: God, Your Father and Creator. Jesus came to restore you to your rightful position and to reveal to you the awesome potential that is trapped inside you.

**Your identity is not found in the
prejudgments of others, but in
the Source from which you came:
God, Your Father and Creator.**

THE THIRD WORLD

*My people will live in peaceful dwelling places, in
secure homes, in undisturbed places of rest*
(Isaiah 32:18).

The wealth within the Third World must be realized, harnessed, and maximized by its people. We must be willing to work and commit ourselves to tapping the potential within the land, our youth, the arts, sports, and music. Our governments must believe that they have the ability to improve on systems and forms institutionalized by the industrialized states. The Church in the Third World must begin to take responsibility for its own people and appreciate that they have the potential to write their own songs and books and to develop an indigenous curriculum for Christian education, leadership training, resource management, and financial autonomy and accountability.

It is crucial that we do not inhibit our potential to chart a new course for the future by being destroyed by our preoccupation with the past. We have the responsibility to deposit the wealth of our potential in this generation so the next generation can build their future on our faithfulness to becoming everything we can possibly be. Just as there is a forest in every seed, so I am certain there is a new world within your world. Whatever God calls for, He provides for.

**I am certain there is a
new world within your world.**

75

BURIED BENEATH

He reveals the deep things of darkness and brings
utter darkness into the light (Job 12:22).

The wealthiest spot on this planet is not the oil fields of Kuwait, Iraq or Saudi Arabia. Neither is it the gold and diamond mines of South Africa, the uranium mines of the Soviet Union, or the silver mines of Africa. Though it may surprise you, the richest deposits on our planet lie just a few blocks from your house. They rest in your local cemetery or graveyard. Buried beneath the soil within the walls of those sacred grounds are dreams that never came to pass, songs that were never sung, books that were never written, paintings that never filled a canvas, ideas that were never shared, visions that never became reality, inventions that were never designed, plans that never went beyond the drawing board of the mind, and purposes that were never fulfilled. Our graveyards are filled with potential that remained potential. *What a tragedy!*

Only a minute percentage of the more than 7 billion people on this planet will experience a significant portion of their true potential. Will you be contributing to the wealth of the cemetery? Ask yourself:

Who am I?

Why am I here?

How much potential do I have?

What am I capable of doing?

By what criteria should I measure my ability?

Who sets the standards?

By what process can I maximize my ability?

What are my limitations?

Within the answers to these questions lies the key to a fulfilled, effective life.

One of the greatest tragedies in life is to watch potential die untapped. Many potentially great people never realize their potential because they don't understand the nature and concept of the potential principle. As God has revealed to me the nature of potential, I have received a burden to teach others what I have learned.

There's a wealth of potential in you. I know, because God has shown me the vast store He placed in me. My purpose is to help you understand that potential and then use it to help others. *You* must decide if you are going to rob the world or bless it with the rich resources locked inside.

You are more than what you have done.

GOOD FOR SOMETHING

The Lord has made his salvation known and revealed his righteousness to the nations (Psalm 98:2).

The brilliant summer sun poured its liquid heat on the windswept island of the Caribbean paradise as the old village sculptor made his way to his humble home outside the village center. On his way he passed by a landowner and his field workers who were felling an age-old tree that for generations had provided protection from the scorching sun.

The old sculptor called over the wall, "What will you do with those discarded stumps of wood?"

The reply, "These are good for nothing but firewood. I have no use for this junk."

The old sculptor begged for a piece of the "junk" wood and with care lifted the knotted tree trunk to his shoulders. He staggered into the distance carrying his burdensome treasure. After entering his cottage, the old man placed the jagged piece of tree in the center of the floor. Then, in a seemingly mysterious and ceremonious manner, he walked around his "useless junk." As the old man picked up his hammer and chisel, he attacked the wood as though setting something free from the gnarled, weathered trunk.

The following morning, the sculptor, asleep on the floor, was clutching a beautifully sculptured bird. He had freed the bird from the bondage of the junk wood. Weeks later the landowner came and saw the bird on the cottage's porch and he asked to buy it. Satisfied that he had made an excellent bargain, the man walked away, hugging the bird to his chest. The old sculptor counted the money and said, "Junk is in the eyes of the beholder. Some look, but others see."

Today there are many individuals whose lives are like the old tree. Trapped within them is a beautiful bird of potential that may never fly. Society, like the landowner, sees nothing in them but useless, worthless people on their way to the garbage heap of life. But we must remember that one person's junk is another person's jewel.

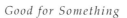

Some look, but others see.

77

REFUSE
TO BE SATISFIED

So let's not get tired of doing what is good. At just the right time we will reap a harvest of blessing if we ***don't give up*** *(Galatians 6:9 NLT).*

Scientists in the field of human potential have estimated that we use as little as 10 percent of our abilities. Therefore, 90 percent of our capabilities lie dormant and wasted. It is sad that we use only a small part of our abilities and talents. Most of us have no idea how much talent and potential we possess.

Consider the life of Abraham Lincoln. His story is one of the most dramatic examples of a man struggling to release the wealth of potential locked up inside him:

- He lost his job in 1832.

- He was elected to the legislature in 1834.

- He suffered the death of his sweetheart in 1834.

- He suffered a nervous breakdown in 1836.

- He was defeated for speaker of the State Legislature in 1838.

- He was defeated for nomination for Congress in 1843.

- He was elected to Congress in 1846.

- He was rejected for the position of land officer in 1849.

- He was defeated for the Senate in 1854.

- He was defeated for the nomination for vice president of the United States in 1856.

- He again was defeated for the Senate in 1858.

- He was elected president of the United States in 1860.

We are responsible for the potential stored within us. We must learn to understand it and effectively use it. Too often our successes prevent us from seeking that which yet lies within us. Success becomes our enemy as we settle for what we have. Refuse to be satisfied with your last accomplishment, because potential never has a retirement plan. Do not let what you *cannot* do interfere with what you *can* do. In essence, what you see is not all there is.

Refuse to be satisfied with your last accomplishment.

78

NOTHING IN LIFE IS INSTANT

When Adam was 130 years old, he became the father of a son who was just like him—in his very image. He named his son Seth. After the birth of Seth, Adam lived another 800 years, and he had other sons and daughters. Adam lived 930 years, and then he died (Genesis 5:3-5 NLT).

Nothing in life is instant. People think miracles are instant, but they really are not. They are just a process that has been sped up. Nothing God created is instant, because God does not operate in the instant. He is a God of the potential principle. Everything begins as potential. He did not create a ready-made human race—the earth was not given an instant population. God made one person—not a million people.

He started with one seed. Then from that one He created another. Then He said to those seeds, "Bless you (that means, 'You have My permission'). Be fruitful and multiply and replenish the earth." In Adam, God gave the earth a seed with the potential of one, one hundred, one thousand, one million…. The seven billion people on the earth today were in that one man. God knew that in Adam and Eve there were enough people to fill the earth. That's the way God works. He knows the potential principle because He introduced it. It is Him.

Potential is always present, waiting to be exposed. It demands that you never settle for what you have accomplished. One of the greatest enemies of your potential is success. God wants you to maximize the potential He has given to you. You are not yet what you are supposed to be—though you may be pleased with what you now are. Don't accept your present state in life as final, because it is just that, a state.

Don't be satisfied—there are many accomplishments yet to be perfected. Since you are full of potential, you should not be the same person next year that you are this year. Never accept an accomplishment as the end—it is only a mark in the process. Because you are God's offspring, there are many selves within you that lie dormant and unused.

**Never accept success as a lifestyle—
it is only a phase.**

79

SUPPOSE...

For I am already being poured out like a drink
offering, and the time for my departure is near.
I have fought the good fight, I have finished
the race, I have kept the faith
(2 Timothy 4:6-7).

Suppose Shakespeare had died before he wrote his poems and plays—the potential of Macbeth would have been buried. Suppose Michelangelo had died before he painted the Sistine Chapel or DaVinci the Mona Lisa—the beauty of their paintings would have been lost. Suppose Mozart had died with all that music in his bosom.

Suppose Moses had died before he saw the burning bush...Paul before he met Jesus on the Damascus Road...Abraham before Isaac was born. How different the pages of Scripture and history would be. Suppose Martin Luther had died without writing the thesis...Charles Wesley without penning the hymns...John Wycliffe without translating the Bible into English. How different the history of the Church might have been.

Can you imagine how many great works of art, music, and literature are buried in the graveyard near your house? Can you imagine how many solutions to the problems we face today are buried with someone you knew? People die without getting out their full potential. They fail to use all that was stored in them for the benefit of the world.

There was a time early in his ministry when the apostle Paul wrote *"For to me, living means living for Christ, and dying is even better. But if I live, I can do more fruitful work for Christ. So I really don't know which is better"* (Philippians 1:21-22 NLT). Though he preferred to die and be with Christ, he knew his purpose in life had not been completely fulfilled. There was yet much fruitful labor for him to do. It was necessary for the Church that he continue to live. Thank God Paul did not die. The benefit of his wisdom would have been lost to the early Church and to us. His potential to write Colossians and Ephesians may have been forfeited.

What would the world have lost if you had not been born?

80

DON'T BE
A ROBBER

*In reply Jesus said: "A man was going down from
Jerusalem to Jericho, when he was attacked by
robbers. They stripped him of his clothes, beat
him and went away, leaving him half dead"*
(Luke 10:30).

Everything in life has the potential to fulfill its
purpose. People who die without achieving
their full potential rob their generation of their
latent ability. Many have robbed me—they've also
robbed you. To die with ability is irresponsible.

Perhaps you are wasting your life doing nothing
with all you have. God packaged some things in
you for the good of the world—use them. We will
never know the wealth God planted in you until
you bring it up. There's always something in you

that we haven't yet seen because that's the way God thinks. Release your ability before you die. Use the power and strength within you for the good of yourself and others. I believe there are books, songs, art works, businesses, poems, inventions, and investments in you that God intended for my children to enjoy. Don't give up until you have lived out the full extent of your potential, because *you have no right to die with my things.*

Don't rob the next generation of the wealth, treasure, and tremendous gifts buried deep within you. If you want to succeed, strike out on new paths. Don't travel the worn paths of accepted success. No one can climb beyond the limitations of their own belief. Every day sends to the grave obscure people who allowed fear to prevent them from realizing their true and full potential. Failure is not the absence of success. Failure is the neglect of trying. What you see is not all there is. There is something in everything.

Principles for discovering the hidden you: God created everything with potential. Nothing in life is instant. Everything in life has the potential to fulfill its purpose. Don't be satisfied with what you now are. Don't die without using your full potential. The greatest threat to progress is your last successful accomplishment.

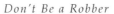

**What you see is not all there is.
There is something more in everything.**

81

FROM
OUT OF GOD

Then God said, "Let us make human beings in our image, to be like us…." So God created human beings in his own image. In the image of God he created them; male and female he created them (Genesis 1:26-27 NLT).

When God created the heavens and the earth, He first decided what He wanted to make something out of and then He spoke to that source. When God wanted plants He spoke to the dirt. When God wanted fish He spoke to the waters. When God wanted animals He spoke to the ground. *Whatever God spoke to became the source from which the created thing came.*

Plants thus came from the dirt, fish from the water and animals from the ground. Furthermore, plants return to the dirt, fish return to the sea and animals return to the ground when they die. All things have the same components and essence as their source. What God created is, in essence, like the substance from which it came. That means plants are 100 percent dirt because they came from dirt. Animals are 100 percent dirt because they came from the ground. If we would take an animal apart, we would come up with genuine dirt. If we would put a plant under a microscope and decipher all the different components, we would find that everything in that plant is in dirt, because the plant is dirt. God called it from the dirt.

Not only are all things composed of that from which they came, they must also remain attached to that source in order to live. All things must be maintained and sustained by where they came from. The minute a plant decides it doesn't like the earth anymore, it dies. The minute the fish decide they are tired of water, they die. The minute animals decide, "We don't want to eat any more dirt," they begin to die.

So, whatever God created came from that to which He spoke: "*God said, 'Let us make human beings in our image, to be like us....' So God created human beings in his own image.*" God created you by speaking to Himself. You came out of God—so you bear His image and likeness.

**God created humans
in His own image.**

82

THE INVENTOR'S INTENTION

But God demonstrates His own love toward us, in
that while we were still sinners, Christ died for us
(Romans 5:8).

Never use the creation to find out who you are, because the purpose of something is only in the mind of the One who made it. That is one of the reasons why God has a tremendous problem with idol worship. How can you identify your ability by worshipping a snake? How can you find out your worth by believing that you will come back as a rat or a roach? How dare you believe that your purpose for existence can be discovered in a relationship with a wooden statue? You will never know yourself by relating to the creation, only to the Creator.

Many inventions would be misunderstood if only the invention were considered and not the intention of the inventor. In other words, the person who created the refrigerator had in his mind what it was supposed to be used for. He didn't intend that it should be used for a trap in the backyard for a kid to be locked in and die from suffocation. Even though thousands of children have died in refrigerators, that was not the inventor's intention.

The automobile is tearing out lampposts all around the world and destroying people's homes and lives. But Henry Ford, who first developed the assembly line to mass produce the automobile, never thought about it that way. He was thinking about transporting people and helping the human race to become a mobile community. He started us to thinking about trolleys and trains and buses. The many people who died through accidents and derailments were not part of his intention. They were not in his mind when he designed his famous T. Ford automobile.

The key to understanding life is in the Source of life, not in life itself.

83

WHAT GOD SEES

Trust in the Lord with all your heart, and lean not on your own understanding (Proverbs 3:5).

Too often we believe the lies we are told. We believe that we are "no good" and worthless. Jesus says, "Not so. I came to show you that you are more than you think you are." You are the image of God.

God always *sees* what people only *look* at. In a manger, God saw a King in a servant, a Savior in a sacrifice, salvation in a crucifixion, a resurrection. In death, God was working at life; in defeat, He was looking at victory. What we look like is not what God sees. God looks beyond the surface to the potential deep within. Beyond the immediate troubles, God sees success, and He continues to call it forth until what He sees becomes reality.

Remember that the seed of every tree is in the fruit of the tree. That means the blessings of the Third World nations are in the Third World nations, and the prosperity of America is in America. When we become concerned about our individual lives or the corporate life of our countries, we come up with all kinds of schemes and plans to solve the problem. But the answer is not in a multitude of systems and programs.

The answer is right inside of us. Our attitudes make the difference. No one can *make you* rowdy or careless or thoughtless. You *are* rowdy and careless and thoughtless because you *choose* to be. So stop it! Stop being rowdy...stop being careless... stop being thoughtless. Only you can control how you act.

God saw in Peter something that Peter had never seen in himself. Peter was so busy agreeing with what others called him that he missed his true potential. When we start believing what others call us, we are in big trouble. Then we throw our hands up in despair and refuse to try. People call us lazy, so we become lazy. People call us careless or stupid or clumsy, so we become careless or stupid or clumsy. Watch it! What others look at is not important. Who we are depends on what *we see*.

**Your attitude makes
all the difference.**

84

A NEW BATTERY

But it was to us that God revealed these things by
his Spirit. For his Spirit searches out everything
and shows us God's deep secrets
(1 Corinthians 2:10 NLT).

Your capped potential is like a new battery. You came into the world full of the ability to run the whole thing. But you're just sitting there. Your stored power isn't being used. Like a battery that needs acidic water inside it before it can really fulfill its purpose, you need something to unleash the potential locked inside you. The Holy Spirit is the key that allows all the dormant power within you to come to life.

As mentioned previously, but is worth repeating, without the filling of the Holy Spirit, you can never function to your fullest potential. The Holy Spirit is the key allowing all the dormant power within you to come to life.

If you just got saved, your spirit doesn't know anything about you. Before your new birth in Christ, you were spiritually dead. Your spirit was paralyzed. You have been unaware of who you really are—because you can't truly know yourself until you become spiritually alive.

If you aren't a Christian, you don't even know who you are. Only your spirit knows the real thoughts of who you are supposed to be—we are born spiritually dead. We will never know who we are supposed to be until we accept Jesus as our Savior and receive God's gift of His Spirit.

King Solomon described this process like a bucket drawing water out of a deep well. The Holy Spirit is the bucket allowing us to understand the wisdom and intentions of our hearts (Proverbs 18:4). God has prepared so many deep things about who we are. Our eyes can't see them, nor can our minds conceive them, yet God is revealing them to us through His Spirit. God doesn't want us to wait until Heaven to know our full potential. God wants us to realize here on this planet who we are. That was His purpose in creating us.

**Do you know
who you really are?**

BORED AND TIRED

For the time will come when people will not put up with sound doctrine. Instead, to suit their own desires, they will gather around them a great number of teachers to say what their itching ears want to hear. They will turn their ears away from the truth and turn aside to myths (2 Timothy 4:3-4).

Many people get bored coming to church. They get tired of singing and tired of praying. Even fasting doesn't meet the hunger of their hearts. Why? Because there's more than coming to church…there's more than singing…there's more than praying. When you hunger for the deep things of God, a hunger that God Himself puts within you, you will not be satisfied until the Holy Spirit reveals God's secret wisdom to you. Your spirit yearns for the deep things of God that He has within Him about you.

There is a deep in you crying out to the deep things in God. You will never be satisfied, even after you are saved, because there is something inside you that continually calls out for more. And the thing you are calling for is locked up in God—the wisdom of God concerning you. You will never be fulfilled until you get filled with what God has that is supposed to be in you. That's why you have to come to God. You'll never be fulfilled without God, because you are looking for what God has.

For this reason, God gives you the Holy Spirit. The only way to get out of God and into you the deep things God knows about you is through His Spirit communing with yours. The Holy Spirit searches the deep things of God—the deep things about you that you lack. God prepared and predestined those things for you before you were created. He had them in Himself and gave them to you at birth. But you don't know those things exist, because sin has capped the well and blocked the way. Only God, through the Holy Spirit, can reveal them again.

You'll never be fulfilled without God, because you are looking for what God has.

86

BACK TO YOUR BEGINNING

How precious to me are your thoughts, God! How vast is the sum of them! (Psalm 139:17)

God wants to take you back to the beginning, because His plans far outreach your plans. His design for your life is so great that King David describes it as *vast* (Psalm 139:17). You are thinking about being a teacher while God wants you to open a school. You have plans to be a clerk while God wants you to own the store. You want to work in a neighboring town while God wants you to go to Africa. You often cheat yourself because you don't realize the potential you have. Why settle to be a doorman when God wants you to own the house? David says it this way: "God, when I look at your thoughts in the book on me, it's like all the sands in the ocean. Your thoughts are endless. I can't fathom your confidence in me."

God designed you to live out the careful plans He prepared for you. You are made in God's image. The plan He wrote for you is perfect and right. Nothing is missing. You have the potential to live out all that God has planned for your life—but only if you accept Jesus Christ as your Savior and Lord. That's the first step toward understanding why you were born.

Though you've messed up God's perfect plan for your life, He offers to write another book for you. It probably won't be the best-seller the first book was designed to be, but at least God gives you the chance to start over. He comes and puts you back in Chapter 1 so you can live the many details of His plan. That's what being born again is all about. It's the opportunity to start over—it's finally getting back to the first chapter of God's book on you. God has great plans for you—that's why He gave you life. Self-acceptance is the key to healthy self-esteem. Accept yourself as God made you.

Allow God's power to transform your weakness to strength.

87

YOUR CREATOR'S DEMANDS AND COMMANDS

*Therefore go and make disciples of all nations,
baptizing them in the name of the Father and of the
Son and of the Holy Spirit, and teaching them to
obey everything I have commanded you. And surely
I am with you always, to the very end of the age*
(Matthew 28:19-20).

Let's think about a flight of the spaceship Chal-
lenger. The people who plan a trip into space
decide before the spaceship ever leaves earth when
the journey will begin, where the spaceship will
go, what the crew will do while in space, how long
the trip will last, and where the ship will land. The
men who created the spaceship and the people who
trained the astronauts know what the ship and the

crew can do. The demands they make are consistent with their potential.

Or suppose you want to take an airplane trip. If you want to fly from Nassau to Chicago, you depend upon the expertise and knowledge of others to assure you that you will get there. You may look at the airplane and say, "This thing will never get me to Chicago," but what you believe doesn't really matter because you are not the creator of either the airplane or the flight route. The folks who build and maintain the airplane would never require it to make the trip from Nassau to Chicago if they thought the plane lacked the potential to do so. The ticket agent would never schedule you for that airplane if the agent knew the flight didn't go to Chicago. The potential of a thing is determined by the demands placed upon it by the creator.

The same is true of your relationship with God. Whenever God demands something of you, don't ask whether you can do it. When you pick up the Bible and read that you can do anything if you believe, don't argue that you can't. God believes—in fact He knows—that whatever you believe hard enough, strong enough, and committed enough can come out of you because He put it in you.

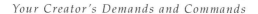

Your potential is determined by the demands of your Creator.

88

DOMINATE THE EARTH

Then God said, "Let us make mankind in our image,
in our likeness, so that they may rule over the fish
in the sea and the birds in the sky, over the livestock
and all the wild animals, and over all the creatures
that move along the ground" (Genesis 1:26).

Your purpose for being is to dominate the earth. (God did not create you to go to church. You go to church because you need to relearn how to live again. Church is school, and when you graduate you will be dead. That's the perfect graduation ceremony—death. Then you finally will come back to who you really are.) You were created to dominate the earth. If God created you and commanded you to dominate the earth, God also is aware that you can do it.

God says, "Dominate the earth."

And you quickly reply, "But, but, but…"

Still God says, "Dominate the earth. I have created you to dominate the earth. I demand that you control, rule, govern, dominate, subdue, and subject this planet."

God wouldn't have made that demand if you couldn't do it. He wired you to dominate this planet. You have the potential to dominate the earth because God placed within every human being the ability to dominate the planet. That is a very serious domination. You dare not complain when you are dominated by the earth (instead of the earth being dominated by you) because God has placed within you the capacity to do whatever He asks. Don't you dare tell God that you cannot do it. He did not give you the responsibility without also giving you the ability. He created you with the ability to dominate the earth.

Dominating the earth is to put God's will first for the benefit of all.

89

ALWAYS
A WAY OUT

*The temptations in your life are no different from what others experience. And **God is faithful. He will not allow the temptation to be more than you can stand. When you are tempted, he will show you a way out** so that you can endure* (1 Corinthians 10:13 NLT).

You have what God demands. God will never demand anything He's not already provided for. Whatever God calls out, He sees. God commanded you to dominate the earth, and you *can*. God never demands anything He's not already provided.

You do not have to be ruled by cocaine, marijuana, or opioids. You do not have to be a victim of alcohol or money or power. God did not create you to be dominated by sex or chemicals. They are nothing but temptations from the evil one. God gives you a way out and you can dominate. The only way to escape these and other dominating habits is to understand your purpose for being.

He did not create you to be *controlled* by anything. He created you so *you could control* the earth.

God looks under all our junk and says what He sees, "You are pure. You are the righteousness of God in Christ Jesus." He looks beneath our unrighteous behavior and sees righteousness. He sees it and calls it out. He'll keep calling it out until it reaches the surface. God's not trying to *make you* into something. He's trying to *expose the real you* He already sees. While you are walking around trying to be good and righteous, God says, "You already are righteous."

He looks beneath your unrighteous behavior and sees righteousness.

90

MOVE ON

*[Jesus says] "If people do not welcome you, **leave
their town and shake the dust off your feet** as a
testimony against them." **So they set out** and went
from village to village, proclaiming the good news
and healing people everywhere* (Luke 9:5-6).

We can climb beyond the limitations we place
on ourselves. Success is not always the result
of our trying. Even Jesus told His disciples to move
on if people don't welcome them. It is courage that
counts—courage and the willingness to try and
then move on. A great deal of talent is lost to the
world because good people lacked a little courage.
Every day sends to the grave, obscure people who
allowed fear and timidity to prevent them from
making their first attempt to do something. Never
tell a person that something can't be done, because

God may have been waiting for centuries for that someone to believe that the impossible is possible.

The poorest of all people are those without a dream. Don't be so afraid of failure that you refuse to try. Demand something of yourself. Failure is only an incident. There's more than the failure—there's success deep behind that failure. Failure is the opportunity to more intelligently begin again. Start again! Learn from it and move on. Don't be paralyzed by what you think is failure.

Failure is proof that you tried. The greatest mistake is being too afraid of making one. People who do nothing in life are usually people who do nothing. If you don't make mistakes, it's usually because you didn't try. Demand things of yourself that are beyond what you have already done. Expect more from yourself than the accomplishments easily within your reach. What you have is not all you are. The limit of your potential is God. I encourage you to attempt something—even though there is a possibility it won't work—than to never try and not know you could have succeeded.

Challenge your potential!

91

YOUR POTENTIAL IS LIMITLESS AND FREE

*If you abide in Me, and My words abide in you, you
will ask what you desire, and it shall be done for you*
(John 15:7 NKJV).

God will give you whatever you ask for as you remain, abide in Him. What a promise! When you open your life completely to God, the Holy Spirit will help you resist every one of satan's attacks. The wealth of your potential is, therefore, limitless and free. Whatever you imagine will be done. God only allows you to think it—because He knows you can do it.

So…the secret to a happy, productive, and abundant life is remaining attached to your Divine Source. If you abide in Christ, His word, His promise will abide in you. You can ask whatever you wish, want, and desire and it will be given to you. God will provide from the depths of His grace... freely, abundantly, victoriously.

You don't have to hustle. You don't have to plead. God is always waiting to help you live a full, fruitful, complete life. From His storehouse of riches, God will supply all you can imagine, and more because He wants you to fulfill your potential. As long as you remain attached to the Vine and submitted to the discipline of the Gardener, you will know God's blessings.

Your potential requires a relationship with its Source. God created you to exalt and bring glory to His name. When you bear fruit, God is glorified. His name is exalted whenever you use the abilities He stored in you. The whole purpose for your being—to reflect and increase the glory of God—is fulfilled when you maximize your potential. God wants His glory to fill the earth through you, His beloved child.

God will supply more of everything than you can imagine!

ABOUT
DR. MYLES MUNROE

(1954–2014)

D R. MYLES MUNROE was more than a pastor, teacher, and author, he was a Christian statesman who became a catalytic thought leader for a whole generation of church leaders and Christ-followers. Dr. Munroe served as a pioneer and prophetic voice, summoning the Church to embrace its heavenly inheritance *now* instead of just holding out for the afterlife.

From the truth-saturated pages of his *Kingdom* book series to his intense international speaking schedule, Dr. Munroe called the global church upward to embrace the holistic message of the Kingdom and discover the culture of Heaven, seeing as much as possible of that Kingdom culture enter into and transform present conditions.

Dr. Munroe's Kingdom message is crucial for the Church today. In an era of great turmoil, uncertainty, and upheaval, Christians need to fully step into their Kingdom purpose. It is not time for Christianity to be intimidated by the encroaching darkness and retreat into hiding. It's time to reveal God's will and purpose on earth as in Heaven. This devotional is a compilation of one of Dr. Munroe's best-selling books, *Understanding Your Potential.*

Dr. Munroe's legacy lives on through Munroe Global, Inc., where his son, Myles Munroe Jr. is the CEO/president and through the Myles and Ruth Munroe Foundation, where their daughter, Charisa, is president. The goal of the ministries is to use the leadership lessons of the late great visionary Dr. Myles Munroe to create new opportunities for people to discover and put into action their life purpose. Also dedicated to the development of nations, one individual at a time, sharing Dr. Munroe's vision to reach the world with priceless principles of leadership and empowerment, spreading the Kingdom Leadership message to the world.

Printed in Great Britain
by Amazon